WRITE BETTER ESSAYS

IN JUST 20 MINUTES A DAY

Elizabeth Chesla

LearningExpress®

NEW YORK

Chesla, Elizabeth L.
    Write better essays in just 20 minutes a day / Elizabeth Chesla—1st ed.
      p. cm.
    ISBN 1-57685-309-8 (pbk.)
    1. English language—Rhetoric—Problems, exercises, etc.   2. Essay—Authorship—
Problems, exercises, etc.   3. Report writing—Problems, exercises, etc.
    I. Title.

PE1471.C47 2000
808'.042—dc21

                                                              00-055651

Printed in the United States of America
9 8 7 6 5 4 3
First Edition

For Further Information

For information on LearningExpress, other LearningExpress products, or bulk sales, please write us at:

    LearningExpress®
    900 Broadway
    Suite 604
    New York, NY 10003

Or visit us at:
    www.learnatest.com

Assignment:	Write an essay that explores one of the many issues raised in *Frankenstein*.
Broad topic:	An issue in *Frankenstein*
Narrowed topic:	Responsibility
Sufficiently narrowed topic:	Responsibility of the creator to his creation
Topic turned into a question:	What is the responsibility of the creator to his creation?
Tentative thesis:	If the creation is a living being, then the creator is responsible for nurturing and educating his "child."

WHEN ASSIGNMENTS ASK QUESTIONS

Some essay assignments are structured in a way that actually can save you a lot of work in narrowing a topic. That is, the assignment itself poses a thesis-bearing question for you. The assignment about television, which was mentioned earlier is a good example:

> *Television is a very powerful medium. What do you think is the ideal place of television in our lives, and why? Explain. How close is the reality to that ideal?*

The two questions are thesis-bearing questions. Below is a student's freewriting response to those questions:

> *I think the ideal place of television is that it should be for information and entertainment but that it shouldn't be watched too much. The reality is far from the ideal because too many people spend too much time watching TV to the point that they don't communicate with each other or do other things that they should be doing to be physically and emotionally healthy (like exercise or do homework).*

This answer is a good tentative thesis. It explains how the student feels about the subject, it responds to the assignment, and it's focused.

PRACTICE 1

Take the following assignment and narrow it down to a question you could turn into a thesis. If you need to do some brainstorming, take a few minutes to freewrite, list, ask questions or map to generate some ideas.

Assignment:	Identify a factor that you believe figures strongly in a child's personality development. Explain how that factor may influence the child.

Broad topic: _____

Narrowed topic: _____

Further narrowed topic: _____

Sufficiently narrowed topic: _____

Topic turned into a question: _____

Tentative thesis: _____

PRACTICE 2

Return to one of your brainstorming sheets from Lesson 3 or 4. Using the four rules of thumb for choosing a topic, narrow down a topic, turn it into a question, and write a tentative thesis.

_____

_____

_____

_____

_____

IN SHORT

To write an effective essay, you need a topic that is interesting to you and that fulfills the assignment. It must also be a topic that is sufficiently focused. Narrow your topic down until you can turn it into a specific question that you can answer. The answer to this question should serve as your _tentative thesis_—the main idea that you will develop in your essay.

Skill Building Until Next Time

Choose topics and develop tentative thesis statements for the other three brainstorming exercises you completed in Lessons 3 and 4.

L·E·S·S·O·N 6

OUTLINING AND ORGANIZATIONAL STRATEGIES

LESSON SUMMARY

This lesson explains the underlying structure of the essay and how to create an outline. You will also learn some of the common organizational strategies writers use.

N ow that you have a tentative thesis, it may be tempting to jump right in and start drafting. And sometimes this approach will work, especially if you've done a lot of brainstorming and have thought carefully about your assignment. More often, however, you'll write a better draft if you first organize your thoughts in an outline.

THE BENEFITS OF AN OUTLINE

Generating an outline before you draft an essay will help you in several ways. First, it will give structure to your ideas. By mapping out the order your ideas should follow, you'll always know where you're headed as you write. This can increase your confidence, speed up the drafting process, and help prevent writer's block.

Second, an outline will help you determine where you need more support for your thesis. When you create an outline, you'll be able to see

if there are any gaps in how you plan to develop your ideas. You'll see where your support is strong and where it is weak.

Third, an outline will help you see whether or not your thesis is tenable. Many writers have written page after page only to discover that their thesis needs to be revised. Sometimes this is unavoidable; after all, writing is a way of discovering and clarifying your thoughts, and you may well change your mind about your topic as you write. But a good outline can help you refine your thesis *before* you begin to draft. Specifically, a good outline will tell you if your thesis is:

- **Too broad.** If you have trouble including everything in your outline, you probably have too much to say. Your thesis needs to be more focused.

- **Too narrow.** If you can't seem to find enough to say, you might have a thesis that's too focused. You need to broaden it a bit.

- **Unreasonable.** If there simply isn't sufficient evidence to support your thesis, you should reconsider its viability. You may need to take a different stance.

- **Underdeveloped.** If you have a lot of gaps in your outline, you may need to do more thinking or research to find sufficient support.

KINDS OF OUTLINES

If you have to drive somewhere you've never been before, you could just jump in the car and drive, hoping your sense of direction will get you there. More likely, though, you'll want to look at a map and write down some directions. But how carefully should you plan your trip? Do you want to map out each fill-up and rest stop? Or do you just want to write down the different route numbers and turns you'll take?

How thoroughly you map out your trip depends upon many different factors, such as your familiarity with the terrain and the distance you need to travel. The same is true in writing. Do you want a detailed, formal outline that lists every major and minor supporting idea, or just a rough, "scratch" outline for your essay? Again, the answer depends upon several different factors, including how comfortable you are with your thesis, how comfortable you are following a structured outline, and how many ideas you've developed through your brainstorming sessions. It also depends upon the writing situation. During a timed essay exam, for example, you don't have the time to write a detailed outline—a rough outline will have to do.

INFORMAL OUTLINES

An informal, rough, or scratch outline is one that generally lists only the major supporting ideas in the order in which you think you should develop them. Here's an example of an informal outline:

> **Assignment:** *Evaluate the proposal to replace the current graded income tax system with a flat tax. Should we institute a flat tax system? Why or why not?*

Tentative thesis: A flat tax would be good for the government and for citizens.
1. Problems with the current tax system
2. How the flat tax works
3. Benefits of the flat tax system
   a. for citizens
   b. for the government

This rough outline provides a general structure for a draft. It's not very detailed—it doesn't include the minor supporting ideas or specific examples the essay needs to be fully developed. But it's certainly enough to get you going and give you a roadmap to follow.

FORMAL OUTLINES

A formal outline, on the other hand, is much more detailed. It should include specific, supporting details and several levels of support. Here's a part of a formal outline for the same assignment:

Tentative thesis: A flat tax would be good for the government and for citizens.
1. Describe problems with the current system
   a. complex
      i. tax rates vary greatly
      ii. too many intricate details
   b. unfair
      i. deductions, loopholes, special interests
      ii. people with same income can pay very different taxes
   c. wasteful
      i. different forms for different people
      ii. huge administrative costs
      iii. huge compliance costs
      iv. advising costs
2. How flat tax works
   a. all citizens pay the same rate—17%—for income over minimum
   b. all citizens get the same personal exemption
   c. no breaks for special interest
   d. no loopholes
3. Benefits
   a. citizens
      i. sense of fairness—all treated equally
      ii. poorest pay no taxes
      iii. simple to calculate and file
      iv. families save more

      v.   *more faith in government*
      vi.   *people will save and invest more*
   b.   *government*
      i.   *streamline IRS*
        (a) *reduce cost*
           (i)   *fewer employees*
           (ii) *less paper, printing, etc., costs*
           (iii) *less auditing costs*
      ii.   *healthier economy*

THE ASSERTION→SUPPORT STRUCTURE

Before moving on to discuss common organizational strategies, it's important to consider the underlying structure of essays. Whether an essay is organized by chronology, comparison and contrast, cause and effect, or some other organizational strategy, every essay has the underlying organizational structure of assertion→support. That is, the essay asserts an idea (its thesis) and then proceeds to support that thesis with specific examples and evidence.

This assertion→support structure is then repeated over and over throughout the essay. The ideas that writers provide to support their thesis (the major supporting ideas) are assertions themselves, and they also need support. *Those* ideas, in turn are assertions as well, and they, too, need support. Thus, the general structure of all essays is really a series of layers of assertions and support:

Main idea (thesis)
    Major supporting idea
        Minor supporting idea
            Support
        Minor supporting idea
            Support
        Minor supporting idea
            Support
    Major supporting idea, and so on.

The exact structure will vary depending upon the number and type of supporting ideas, but this structure is the foundation for most kinds of essays.

COMBINING ORGANIZATIONAL STRUCTURES

It's important to note that all essays actually use a *combination* of organizational structures. While you'll probably use one strategy to organize the essay overall, you'll use other organizational strategies throughout the sup-

porting sections. For example, say your assignment asks you to compare and contrast two characters in a short story. Your overall organizing principle will be the comparison/contrast structure. However, different sections *within* the essay may use other organizational techniques. If you are comparing and contrasting the actions of the two characters, for example, you might also use chronology to describe events. Or you might break down several characteristics of the characters—their education, their upbringing, and their values—and use analysis/classification to organize your ideas. Or you could use cause and effect to compare and contrast why the characters chose to behave as they did.

The rest of this lesson explains three different organizational strategies. Four more will be covered in the next lesson.

COMMON ORGANIZATIONAL STRUCTURES

The *writing* process is also a *decision-making* process. So far you've made two major choices: what to write about and what to say about your topic. Now, it's time to make another important decision: How do you want to organize your information?

There are many different organizational strategies that you can chose from. Some will work better than others depending upon your assignment and material. The more familiar you are with each strategy, the easier it will be for you to create an outline and organize your ideas for your draft.

CHRONOLOGICAL/SEQUENTIAL

One way to organize ideas is by chronology. You can put your ideas in the order in which they did happen, should happen, or will happen. Chronology, or some variation of it (in which, for example, you use flashbacks), is usually the best kind of organization for essays in which you are asked to narrate or describe an experience. Sequential order is the best kind of organization any time you are describing a procedure or instructions, such as the process of photosynthesis or the procedure for passing a bill in Congress. Of course, it's essential that your ideas be in the proper order. Poor chronology or bad sequencing can cause a great deal of confusion.

Here's a sample rough outline using chronology as its main organizing principle:

Assignment: Describe a time when you and a family member experienced a deep sense of conflict or when you sharply disagreed about an important issue. What caused the conflict? What was the outcome? Have your feelings about the matter changed or remained the same? Explain.

Tentative thesis: When I decided to become a vegetarian, my parents refused to support me. It was very difficult to stick to my decision—but I'm glad I did.

Rough Outline:

1. *Telling my family*
2. *Their reactions*
3. *Trying to explain my reasons*

4. *Flashback: taking the "virtual tour" of the slaughterhouse on the Web*

5. *Offering to take family on the tour, but only Jenny watching it with me*

6. *Mom and Dad refusing to cook special meals for me*

7. *Learning how to cook for myself*

8. *Jenny accepting my decision and trying some vegetarian food with me*

9. *Jenny giving up meat too*

10. *Mom and Dad accepting our decision and supporting us*

PRACTICE 1

On a separate sheet of paper or your computer, create an outline using chronology as your main organizing principle. Your outline can be rough or formal. Use one of your own brainstorms from Lesson 3 or 4 or one of the brainstorms provided as examples to create your outline.

CAUSE AND EFFECT

Another way to organize ideas is by cause and effect. You can move from the cause to the effect or from the effect to the cause:

1. cause➔effect: what happened (cause) and what happened as a result (effect)

2. effect➔cause: what happened (effect) and why it happened (cause)

Like chronology, cause and effect can be the main organizational structure of the whole essay or it can be used to organize specific parts. It can also be used in combination with other organizing principles. For example, if your assignment is to discuss the events that led to World War I, you would probably use cause and effect as well as chronology to organize your ideas.

> **NOTE**: Whenever you write about cause and effect, keep in mind that most events have more than one cause, and most actions generate more than one effect.

Here's a part of an outline for an essay about the effect of the Industrial Revolution on city life:

Industries moved to cities
> *Large influx of working class from rural areas looking for jobs*
>> *Crowded, unsanitary conditions*
>> *Children in the streets (unsupervised) or working in factories (uneducated)*
> *Demand for more hospitals, police, sanitation, social services*

SPATIAL

Ideas can also be organized according to spatial principles: from top to bottom, side to side, inside to outside, and so on. This organizing principle is particularly useful when you are describing an item or place. You'd use this strategy, for example, to describe the structure of an animal or plant, the room where an important event took place, or a place that is important to you.

The key to this organizing principle is that you move around the space or object logically; don't jump around. Below is a rough outline for an essay using the spatial organizing principle. The student works from the outside of a cell to the inside to describe its structure:

Structure of an animal cell:
1. *Plasma membrane*
   a. *Isolates cytoplasm*
   b. *Regulates flow of materials between cytoplasm and environment*
   c. *Allows interaction with other cells*
2. *Cytoplasm*
   a. *Contains water, salt, enzymes, proteins*
   b. *Also contains organelles like mitochondria*
3. *Nuclear envelope*
   a. *Protects nucleus*
4. *Nucleus*
   a. *Contains cell's DNA*

PRACTICE 2

On a separate sheet of paper or your computer, create an outline using either the cause and effect or spatial organizing principles. Your outline can be formal or informal. Use one of your own brainstorms from Lesson 3 or 4 or one of the brainstorms provided as examples to create your outline.

IN SHORT

Creating an outline before you begin to draft an essay can make your drafting process much more productive and effective. You'll have a road map to follow as you draft and you will be able to see where your ideas need more development. Underlying all essays is the assertion→support structure. Beyond that, you can organize ideas by chronology (time), cause and effect, or spatial arrangement.

Skill Building Until Next Time

In a well-organized essay, the writer's organizing principle should be very clear. Look for essays or parts of essays that you think are organized by chronology, cause and effect, or spatial principles. Develop an outline from the text so that you can see the organizational structure more clearly.

L·E·S·S·O·N

MORE ORGANIZATIONAL STRATEGIES

7

LESSON SUMMARY

This lesson describes four more organizational strategies for essays: analysis/classification, order of importance, compare and contrast, and problem→solution.

I n the previous lesson, you learned ways to organize ideas according to time and space. Now you'll examine four additional principles of organization:

- analysis/classification
- order of importance
- compare and contrast
- problem→solution

ANALYSIS/CLASSIFICATION

Some essays are best organized by analysis or classification, where you arrange items, ideas, or events by their characteristics or functions. For example, look at the following assignment:

Plants and animals protect themselves in many different ways. Describe the various strategies organisms have developed for protection.

Because there are many different strategies you could describe, your best bet is probably to group similar strategies together and organize your essay by type (classification). Thus, a detailed outline for your essay might look like the following:

1. *appearance*
   a. *camouflage*
      i. *moths*
      ii. *flounder*
      iii. *walking stick*
   b. *warning colors*
      i. *monarch butterfly*
      ii. *coral snake*
      iii. *South American poisonous frog*
   c. *mimicry*
      i. *king snake resembling coral snake*
      ii. *swallowtail butterfly larva resembling snake*
      iii. *snowberry fly resembling jumping spider*
2. *chemicals*
   a. *smoke*
      i. *squid*
      ii. *octopus*
   b. *smells*
      i. *skunks*
      ii. *others?*
   c. *poisons*
      i. *spiders*
      ii. *snakes*
      iii. *bombardier beetles*
3. *armor*
   a. *spikes, thorns*
      i. *roses and thistles*
      ii. *sea urchins*
      iii. *porcupines*
   b. *shells, hard coverings*
      i. *nuts*
      ii. *beetles*
      iii. *turtles*

Notice how the strategies are first classified into three categories: appearance, chemicals, and armor. Each of these three categories is then further classified for analysis. Appearance, for example, is broken down into three types of protection strategies involving appearance: camouflage, warning colors, and mimicry.

ORDER OF IMPORTANCE

One of the most frequently used organizational strategies is order of importance. It's often the main organizing principle, and even when it's not, it's often used throughout an essay in individual sections and paragraphs.

Order of importance means that you rank ideas from most important to least important, or least important to most important. "Most important" generally means most *supportive*, most *convincing*, or most *striking*. For example, the outline above lists several strategies that plants and animals use for protection. While the overall organizing principle is analysis/classification, most sections within that larger structure are also organized by order of importance. Look again, for example, at the section on appearance:

1. appearance
   a. camouflage
      i. moths
      ii. flounder
      iii. walking stick
   b. warning colors
      i. monarch butterfly
      ii. coral snake
      iii. South American poisonous frog
   c. mimicry
      i. king snake resembling coral snake
      ii. swallowtail butterfly larva resembling snake
      iii. snowberry fly resembling jumping spider

"Appearance" is one of the essay's major supporting ideas. The three minor supporting ideas for "appearance"—camouflage, warning colors, and mimicry—are listed in order of importance. Camouflage is the most common and least sophisticated of the three, whereas mimicry is the most unique and most compelling way that animals use appearance to protect themselves. And for each of these three supporting ideas, three specific examples are provided. Again, they are listed in order of importance, from the least striking example to the most compelling.

Whenever you're building an argument (and in most essays that's exactly what you're doing), your essay will be more effective if you start with the least important idea and move to the most important. A good argument is like a snowball rolling down a hill. It builds in momentum and strength as it rolls, one idea building upon another. And because you're working to convince readers that your assertions are valid, it helps to use this

structure. Your least important ideas are probably also the least controversial and are therefore easiest to accept. Better to start this way and have your reader agree with some of what you say before you bring up points that may be more difficult to accept.

Of course, what one person considers "most important" may not be what others consider most important. For example, imagine you are arguing that the U.S. shouldn't have dropped the atomic bomb on Hiroshima. You have three major supporting ideas:

The bomb wasn't necessary to end the war.
The bomb was dropped for political, not military, reasons.
The bomb killed hundreds of thousands of innocent people.

You might feel that the most important issue is civilian casualties; someone else might feel that the most important issue is the government's motivation. Your outlines and essays will therefore be considerably different. What's important is that your organization corresponds with your thesis and helps you build your case.

PRACTICE 1

On a separate sheet of paper or your computer, create an outline using analysis/classification or order of importance as your main organizing principle. Your outline can be rough or formal. Use one of your own brainstorms from Lesson 3 or 4 or one of the brainstorms provided as examples to create your outline.

COMPARISON AND CONTRAST

Essays that show the similarities and differences between two or more items use the comparison and contrast organizational strategy.

A good comparison and contrast essay depends upon having comparable items. For example, you'd have difficulty writing a successful essay if you wanted to compare Frankenstein's creature with Cinderella. Frankenstein's creature and Pinocchio, on the other hand, *are* comparable items—they're both beings that someone else brought to life. With comparable items, you can then select the aspects of those items you wish to compare and contrast. For example, you could compare and contrast the (1) creation of these beings, (2) their creator's reactions after they come to life, and (3) their relationship to their creator.

After you've selected the aspects to compare, there are two ways you can organize your discussion: the block technique and the point-by-point technique.

THE BLOCK TECHNIQUE

The block technique organizes ideas by **item** (A and B). First, discuss all of the aspects of item A (A1, A2, A3). Then discuss all of the corresponding aspects of item B (B1, B2, B3). The result is two "blocks" of text—a section about item A, and a section about item B. For example:

(*A = Pinocchio; B = Frankenstein's creature*)

A1—Pinocchio's creation

A2—Geppetto's reaction

A3—Relationship between Pinocchio and Geppetto

B1—The creature's creation

B2—Frankenstein's reaction to his creation

B3—Relationship between Frankenstein and his creature

THE POINT-BY-POINT TECHNIQUE

The point-by-point method organizes ideas by **aspect** (1, 2, 3) rather than item, so the result is a direct comparison and contrast of each aspect. Because you put each aspect side by side, readers get to see exactly how the two items measure up, element by element. This is a more sophisticated way of organizing a comparison and contrast essay and is a little more reader friendly. Here's a sample outline:

A1—Pinocchio's creation

B1—The creature's creation

A2—Geppetto's reaction

B2—Frankenstein's reaction

A3—Relationship between Pinocchio and Geppetto

B3—Relationship between Frankenstein and his creature

PROBLEM→SOLUTION

Finally, another way to organize your ideas is to identify the problem and then offer a solution.

Unlike other formats, which can often be flexible (chronological order, for example, can be interrupted by flashbacks), there's little room for flexibility in this structure. The problem must come first so that readers understand exactly what the solution solves. Again, this strategy is often combined with other organizational strategies. When problem→solution is the main organizing principle, it will also often use cause and effect, analysis/

classification, chronology or order of importance as well. Here's the "solution" section of an outline for an essay about the problem of misinformation on the Internet:

B. Solution
1. Create "Reliability Index"
   a. Ranks sites for level of credibility
   b. Run by not-for-profit; perhaps university or consortium of universities
   c. Organization would rate Web sites on scale of trustworthiness (fact-check, etc.)
      i. Priorities:
         1. Sites offering information about health and health care
         2. Sites offering information about raising children (education, emotional and social development)
         3. Sites offering information about finances and investments

2. Run awareness campaign
   a. Public service announcements
   b. Lessons in schools
   c. Announcements by all Internet providers

PRACTICE 2

On a separate sheet of paper or your computer, create an outline using comparison and contrast or problem-solution as your main organizing principle. Your outline can be rough or formal. Use one of your own brainstorms from Lesson 3 or 4 or one of the brainstorms provided as examples to create your outline.

IN SHORT

Analysis, order of importance, comparison and contrast and problem→solution are four more strategies to help you organize your ideas for an essay. One strategy will generally serve as your overall organizing principle, while other strategies will help you organize individual paragraphs and sections of your essay.

Skill Building Until Next Time

Look for essays or parts of essays that you think use the analysis/classification, comparison and contrast, order of importance, or problem→solution strategies for organization. Work backwards from the text to create an outline so you can see the organizing structure more clearly.

S·E·C·T·I·O·N
DRAFTING THE ESSAY

Now that you've done some planning, you're warmed up and ready to run. The lessons in this section will show you how to draft a successful essay, from introduction to conclusion.

L · E · S · S · O · N 8

THESIS STATEMENTS AND THE DRAFTING PROCESS

LESSON SUMMARY

This lesson explains the drafting process and how to draft a thesis statement. You'll learn what makes a strong thesis statement and what kinds of approaches to avoid.

I f it seems like you've done a lot of work already, that's because you have. In the planning stage, you made several very important decisions and took several steps to give yourself the materials you need for a good draft. You broke down the assignment, brainstormed ideas, focused your topic, developed a tentative thesis, *and* sketched an outline. Now you're ready to write a draft.

WHAT IT MEANS TO DRAFT

To *draft* means to create a preliminary version or rough form of a text. "Preliminary" and "rough" are key words for successful drafting. Like brainstorming, drafting is most effective if you allow yourself to write imperfectly. The idea, especially for your first draft, is to just get your ideas down on paper. You don't have to worry about saying it just right. Just say it. You can make notes to yourself, like "explain more" or "add stuff about X here." You will have plenty of time to expand and refine your ideas and correct mistakes later. You can use slang, clichés, and other stylistic no-

no's you'd eliminate during the revision process. You can even leave sections blank and go back to them later. Save precision for the revision process. A draft is a place for approximation.

Many writers have sat down, thesis and outline in hand, ready to draft, only to stare at a blank page for hours and hours without writing a word. Why? Because they don't know how to begin. They want to start with a good, solid introduction that will give them momentum and carry them through the essay. Instead, they waste time and end up feeling frustrated with the whole writing process.

Your introduction presents readers with your topic and thesis and should draw readers into your essay, so it's important that your introduction be powerful and effective. But your first draft is not necessarily the time to worry about your introduction. If you know how you want to introduce your essay, fine; but if you don't, don't worry about it. Just jump right into the body of your essay and start developing your first major idea. *You don't have to start with the introduction.* That can come later, after you've gotten your ideas out and have a much clearer idea of what you're saying. (That's why the lesson on introductions doesn't appear until *after* the lessons on writing good paragraphs and providing support.)

Tips for Overcoming Writer's Block

Don't know what to say? Try one of the brainstorming techniques described in Lessons 3 and 4.

Don't know where to begin? Create an outline. This will help you put your ideas in order and give you a "road map" to follow.

Can't think of the right way to start? Skip the introduction and jump right in. There's no rule that says you have to start at the beginning. Once you know where you're going and what you have to say, you can come back and craft an effective introduction.

HOW MANY DRAFTS SHOULD YOU WRITE?

There's no rule about how many drafts you should write. The number of drafts will vary from essay to essay, depending upon several different factors, such as how detailed your outline is and how comfortable you are with the material. But as a general rule, unless you're extremely lucky—or unless you've just plain run out of time— you'll want to write more than one draft of your essay. In fact, once you become accustomed to the drafting process, you'll probably find yourself writing *more* drafts than you used to because it's actually easier to get your ideas out and then refine them through a series of rough drafts. This may sound like it takes more time, but consider how much time you might otherwise spend staring at a blank page or being stuck in the middle of a sentence because you just don't know how to say it right. In the end, more drafts usually mean more productive writing time and a much better essay.

TIPS FOR THE DRAFTING PROCESS

Use the following guidelines to help keep your ideas flowing through the drafting stage:

- **Keep your thesis statement and assignment in front of you at all times.** This will help you stay focused on what you need to do in your essay.
- **Follow your outline, but be flexible.** Don't feel obligated to stick to your original plan. You may decide as you're writing that a different order of ideas makes more sense.
- **Save your drafts.** Whether they're on paper or on the computer, keep a copy of every version of your essay. You may find that an idea you thought you weren't going to use will have a place in your essay after all. (If you don't want to have a lot of files on your computer or disk, print out each draft before you write over it.)

PRACTICE 1

Briefly describe your typical writing process. How have you typically handled drafting in the past? What can you do to make drafting more productive?

_____

_____

_____

_____

_____

DRAFTING A THESIS STATEMENT

While you don't need to start with an introduction, you *do* need to have a pretty good idea of your thesis before you begin to draft. The best way to do that is to draft a thesis statement.

In Lesson 5, you learned how to narrow your topic and formulate a tentative thesis. Your thesis is the main idea of your essay, the idea that the rest of your essay will develop and support. A strong thesis is vital for an effective essay.

A thesis statement is simply the sentence or sentences that express your thesis. A good thesis statement tells your reader the subject of your essay and your position on the subject (the main idea that you will develop). It may also suggest the structure of your essay. Here are three explanations for what a strong thesis statement is.

1. A good thesis statement makes a strong, clear assertion that clearly conveys *your* attitude about the subject.

    No assertion: *Dr. Strangelove* is about the cold war.

    Mild assertion: *Dr. Strangelove* is an interesting film about the absurdity of the cold war.

    Strong assertion: *Dr. Strangelove* is a scathing indictment of American nuclear strategy and cold war politics.

2.   A strong thesis statement is focused. If it is too broad, you will not be able to develop your ideas in sufficient depth because there will be too much material to cover.

Too broad: Animals have developed many strategies for survival.

Some focus: Animals have developed many strategies to protect themselves.

Focused: Many animals have developed physical properties that serve to protect them from predators.

3.   A good thesis statement is not too narrow. While your thesis needs to be focused, it still has to be general enough to be supported with details, specific examples, facts, and so on.

Too narrow: In "The Open Boat," the repetition of "If I am going to be drowned" conveys Crane's theme of the indifference of nature.

Focused, but not too narrow: In "The Open Boat," Crane uses several stylistic techniques to convey his theme of the indifference of nature.

That's what a thesis statement is. Now, here is what a thesis statement is not:

1.   A thesis statement is **NOT** simply an announcement of the subject matter. You still need to tell readers what you are going to say *about* your subject.

Announcement: "This paper will discuss the dropping of the atomic bomb on Hiroshima."

Thesis statement: "The U.S. was wrong to drop the atomic bomb on Hiroshima."

2.   A thesis statement is **NOT** simply a question or list of questions. You still need to tell your readers what *idea* you are going to develop in your essay (the answer to one or more of your questions).

Question: Why did Kafka choose to turn Gregor into a giant beetle?

Thesis statement: Gregor's transformation into a giant beetle is a powerful symbol representing Gregor's industrial nature, his role within his family before his transformation, and his status with the family after his transformation.

Note: This thesis statement also tells the reader the structure that the essay will follow. It lays out the three symbolic meanings in the order in which they will be developed in the essay.

3.   A thesis statement is **NOT** simply a statement of fact. It must be an assertion that conveys your ideas about the subject.

Statement of fact: There are many important similarities between the Perrault and Grimm versions of "Little Red Riding Hood."

Thesis statement: Both the Perrault and Grimm Brothers versions of "Little Red Riding Hood" reveal the authors' negative attitudes towards women.

WHERE YOUR THESIS STATEMENT BELONGS

While there's no rule that states exactly where your thesis statement should go, in general, your thesis statement should come early in your essay. Writers often find the best place for a thesis statement is at or near the end of their introductory paragraph or paragraphs, though the exact placement of the thesis statement will vary from essay to essay. What's important is that readers know before they get too far into your essay what idea you will be developing. Think of it this way: Imagine that someone you don't know calls you on the phone. After she introduces herself, you expect that she will tell you *why* she's calling. What does she want? If she doesn't tell you, you'll be annoyed, perhaps even suspicious or angry. You deserve the courtesy of an explanation, don't you? So do your readers. Their "explanation" comes in the form of your thesis statement.

While you should have a good working thesis statement to drive you through your draft, it's important to remember that even your thesis statement is a draft. It's your preliminary version—and as you write and discover through writing, this statement is bound to undergo some revision, too. So be flexible. Better to revise your thesis statement to fit what you've written in your essay than to revise your whole essay to fit your thesis.

PRACTICE 2

Revise the following weak thesis statements to make them strong.

1. In this essay, I will explain why I want to attend Briarwood College.

    _____

    _____

2. The death penalty is a controversial issue.

    _____

    _____

3. This novel had an important impact on my life.

    _____

    _____

4. What would the consequences of censorship on the Internet be?

    _____

    _____

PRACTICE 3

Draft thesis statements for two of the assignments for which you developed outlines in Lessons 6 and 7.

_____

_____

_____

_____

IN SHORT

Drafts are _rough_ versions of your essay—a chance to get your ideas out so that you can shape them into an effective essay. To get started, draft a thesis statement that makes a strong assertion about your subject. Be sure it's focused and avoid simply making an announcement, asking a question, or stating a fact.

Skill Building Until Next Time

Read through several essays and look for their thesis statements. How do the authors convey their main idea? Where is the thesis statement located?

PARAGRAPHS AND TOPIC SENTENCES

LESSON SUMMARY

This lesson explains what makes a good paragraph. You'll learn about topic sentences and paragraphing formats.

Imagine opening up a novel and seeing that the entire text is one giant paragraph. How would you feel? You'd probably feel pretty overwhelmed and more than a little annoyed with the author. Why didn't he break the text into paragraphs? How are you going to know when he shifts from idea to idea? How inconsiderate. And how your eyes will burn as you read!

Paragraphs are so central to good writing that we tend to take them for granted. But it's worth reviewing their function and recognizing the important benefits they provide.

WHAT ARE PARAGRAPHS?

Paragraphs are one of a writer's most important tools. By definition, a paragraph is one or more sentences about a single idea. We indicate a paragraph by indenting the first line or adding a line break at the end of the paragraph. By clustering a group of related sentences together like this,

paragraphs divide text into manageable chunks of information. Paragraphs are like punctuation for the eye; they visually separate ideas for your readers.

Like essays, paragraphs generally have three parts:

- a **beginning (introduction)** which introduces the topic of the paragraph and often expresses the main idea of that paragraph in a topic sentence
- a **middle (body)** which develops and supports the main idea
- an **end (conclusion)** which expresses the main idea of the paragraph, if it wasn't expressed in the introduction; offers concluding thoughts about that topic; and/or offers a transition to the next paragraph.

Here's an example of a complete paragraph:

> *The African country of the Democratic Republic of Congo has had a turbulent past. It was colonized by Belgium in the late nineteenth century and officially declared a Belgian territory by King Leopold in 1895. The country, called the Belgian Congo after 1908, was under Belgian rule for 65 years. Then, in 1960, after several years of unrest, Congo was granted independence from Belgium. The country was unstable for several years. Two presidents were elected and deposed, and there was much arguing over who should run the country and how. Finally, in 1965, a man named Mobutu Sese Seko rose to power. Though the country was remarkably rich in resources such as diamonds, under Sese Seko's rule the people of Zaire lived in complete squalor. Still, Sese Seko brought some stability to the region. He ruled for 32 years, until the people finally rebelled in 1997.*

The first sentence in the paragraph introduces the topic and expresses its main idea; it is the paragraph's topic sentence. The next seven sentences develop and support that idea. Then, the last two sentences conclude the paragraph nicely. They remind readers of the main idea of the paragraph (the country's unstable past) and leads them into the next paragraph by introducing the 1997 rebellion that removed Sese Seko from power.

DEVELOPING STRONG PARAGRAPHS

Paragraphs are the essay in microcosm. Just as an essay is driven by one main idea (its thesis), a good paragraph is also held together by one controlling idea. This idea is usually stated in a topic sentence.

TOPIC SENTENCES

Topic sentences are like mini thesis statements. Just as your thesis statement expresses the main idea of your essay, topic sentences express the main idea of each paragraph. Like a thesis, this main idea must:

1. Make an assertion about the subject. This assertion can be fact or opinion. Here are examples of each.

    Fact: Another strategy plants and animals use to protect themselves is mimicry.

    Opinion: The most interesting strategy plants and animals have developed for protection is mimicry.

2. Be general enough to encompass all of the ideas in the passage. If it isn't, then the paragraph is probably trying to do too much.

It's logical to begin a paragraph with the topic sentence, but there's no rule that says that's where the topic sentence has to go. Typically, you'll find the topic sentence at the beginning of a **deductive** paragraph. In an **inductive** paragraph, the topic sentence is usually found at the end of the paragraph.

DEDUCTIVE AND INDUCTIVE FORMATS

There are two main ways of organizing paragraphs: deductively and inductively. These two structures are based on the deductive and inductive reasoning strategies in the field of logic.

Deductive Paragraphs

In a deductive argument, you are first presented with a "conclusion"—the main argument or claim being made about the subject. Then you are given the evidence that supports the conclusion. This structure also works well for the paragraph. In many paragraphs, you are first presented with a **general** idea (usually expressed in a topic sentence). That general idea is then followed by **specific** examples which support that idea.

Here's an example of a deductive paragraph:

I could tell the test results just by the look on his face. He couldn't bring himself to look at me. The blood had drained out of his face and he was as pale as china. He tried to smile but the corners of his mouth refused to co-operate. His shoulders drooped and his whole body seemed to buckle under the weight of the news, as if he'd already given up his fight against the disease.

Notice how the paragraph begins with a topic sentence that expresses the main idea—that his look revealed the test result. The rest of the paragraph gives specific details about his expression to "prove" that main idea. (Of course, this is the same general structure you can use for essays.)

Inductive Paragraphs

Inductively organized paragraphs, on the other hand, like their inductive argument counterparts, *begin* with the specific examples and lead up to a general idea (the "conclusion," usually expressed in a topic sentence). They present the evidence first, then the conclusion that's drawn from that evidence. Here's an example:

All day she counted pills and put them in vials. Scoop after scoop, she measured out doses of medicine. Drip by drip, she prepared solutions for the sick and weary. She knew her job was important, but the monotony made her long for a job that was more exciting.

This paragraph starts by giving us specific "evidence." Then, in a topic sentence at the end of the paragraph, the writer offers the conclusion she has drawn from that evidence.

Of course, not all paragraphs will fit so neatly into the general→specific (deductive) or specific→general (inductive) formats, and not all paragraphs will have a topic sentence either at the beginning or end of the paragraph. But most paragraphs do, and these two structures form the backbone of paragraphing strategy.

HOW LONG SHOULD A PARAGRAPH BE?

There's no specific rule about how long a paragraph should be. But there are some guidelines you should follow:

Long paragraphs are hard on the eye; use them sparingly. If you've written a page or more without a break, take a careful look at your ideas. Can they be broken up in a logical way? To be reader friendly, a typical typed page should have at least one paragraph break, preferably two to four.

Very short paragraphs, on the other hand, look underdeveloped, like incomplete thoughts. They should only be used if you have a sentence (or two) that is important enough to be on its own. A one-sentence paragraph has impact. It stands out visually, and the pauses before and after the sentence give it more time to sink in and take hold. A one- or two-sentence paragraph should only come along once in a while, though—maybe once a page, if that often.

Here's the Congo paragraph from above, revised to include a very short paragraph:

> The African country of the Democratic Republic of Congo has had a turbulent past. It was colonized by Belgium in the late nineteenth century and officially declared a Belgian territory by King Leopold in 1895. The country, called the Belgian Congo after 1908, was under Belgian rule for 65 years. Then, in 1960, after several years of unrest, Congo was granted independence from Belgium.

> But independence came at a price.

> For the next five years, the Congo experienced political and social turmoil. Two presidents were elected and deposed, and there was much arguing over who should run the country and how. Finally, in 1965, a man named Mobutu Sese Seko rose to power. Though the country was remarkably rich in resources such as diamonds, under Sese Seko's rule the people of Zaire lived in complete squalor. Still, Sese Seko brought some stability to the region. He ruled for 32 years, until the people finally rebelled in 1997.

Notice how sharply the second paragraph stands out. By allowing that sentence to stand alone, the writer has underscored her emphasis on the cost of independence for the Republic of Congo.

PRACTICE 1

Divide the following text into paragraphs. Underline the topic sentences in each paragraph you create.

> Sigmund Freud, the father of psychoanalysis, made many contributions to the science of psychology. One of his greatest contributions was his theory of the personality. According to Freud, the human personality is made up of three parts: the id, the ego, and the superego. The id is the part of the personality that exists only in the subconscious. According to Freud, the id has no direct contact with reality. It is the innermost core of our personality and operates according to the pleasure principle. That is, it seeks immediate gratification for its desires, regardless of eternal realities or consequences. It is not even aware that external realities or consequences exist.

The ego develops from the id and is the part of the personality in contact with the real world. The ego is conscious and therefore aims to satisfy the subconscious desires of the id as best it can within the individual's environment. When it can't satisfy those desires, it tries to control or suppress the id. The ego functions according to the reality principle. The superego is the third and final part of the personality to develop. This is the part of the personality that contains our moral values and ideals, our notion of what's right and wrong. The superego gives us the "rules" that help the ego control the id. For example, a child wants a toy that belongs to another child (id). He checks his environment to see if it's possible to take that toy (ego). He can, and does. But then he remembers that it's wrong to take something that belongs to someone else (superego) and returns the toy to the other child.

PRACTICE 2

Write topic sentences for the following paragraphs. Make at least one paragraph deductive (place the topic sentence at the beginning of the paragraph) and at least one paragraph inductive (place the topic sentence at the end of the paragraph).

1. The government's Bureau of Labor Statistics (BLS) reports that employment in health service industries through the year 2005 will grow at almost double the rate of all other (non-farm) wage and salary employment. In sheer numbers, about 9 million American workers are now employed in health services. By 2005, that number is expected to be at about 13 million—an increase of nearly 4 million jobs.

2. When I was in kindergarten, I wanted to be an astronaut. When I was in junior high school, I wanted to be a doctor. When I was in high school, I wanted to be a teacher. Today, I'm 35 and I'm a firefighter.

3. The proposed tax referendum will not reduce taxes for middle income families. In fact, middle income families with children will pay 10 percent *more* per year, and families without children will pay 20 percent more. Further, the referendum actually *decreases* taxes for the wealthiest tax bracket. In fact, taxpayers in the highest income bracket will pay 10 percent less per year if the referendum is passed.

IN SHORT

A paragraph is a group of sentences about one idea. That idea is usually expressed in a topic sentence. Deductive paragraphs begin with the topic sentence and then provide specific examples or support. Inductive paragraphs begin with the examples or evidence and then state the main idea. Avoid long paragraphs, which are hard on the eye and often difficult to follow. Use one or two sentence paragraphs occasionally to make an important idea stand out.

Skill Building Until Next Time

As you read, pay particular attention to paragraphing. When do writers begin new paragraphs? Why? Can you identify topic sentences? Do you recognize inductive or deductive formats?

L·E·S·S·O·N

PROVIDING SUPPORT

10

LESSON SUMMARY

As important as your thesis is the evidence that supports it. This lesson describes six different strategies for supporting your assertions.

Back in Lesson 1, the word "friendly" was used to describe the "general reader." And it's important to think of your reader in this way. It helps you to relax and it lessens the temptation to be defensive or adversarial. But just because your reader is friendly doesn't mean she has to accept everything you say. In fact, it's wise to think of your reader as friendly, but skeptical. She will listen politely but at the same time demand evidence for your assertions. She's not just going to take your word for it. Nor should she. An essay, after all, is an exercise in explanation. As essay tells readers, "Here is what I think, and here is *why* I think it."

Fortunately, there are many different types of support you can provide for your readers. Most types of support fit into one of six categories:

- specific examples
- facts
- reasons
- descriptions and anecdotes
- expert opinion and analysis
- quotations from the text

The boundaries of these categories are not absolute; for example, a specific example is often a fact or an anecdote. These categories, however, are useful for discussing types of support and providing a wide range of examples in this lesson.

SPECIFIC EXAMPLES

The broadest category of evidence is specific examples. A specific example offers something tangible to your readers. It gives concrete evidence of your assertion; it is a person, place or thing that illustrates your idea. For example, imagine that you've drafted the following thesis statement:

Recent movies have portrayed the American suburb as a place of false happiness and hidden misery. But this is an unfair and inaccurate depiction.

With this thesis, you have two ideas to support: first, that this is how recent films have portrayed the American suburb; and second, that this is an unfair and inaccurate depiction. For your first idea, you should provide specific examples of movies that are guilty of this portrayal. You could cite *American Beauty* and *The Ice Storm*—two highly acclaimed films—as specific examples.

Of course, you need to do more than simply name the films if you want your essay to be convincing. For each of these specific examples, you need to demonstrate that each film portrays the American suburb in this negative way. Thus, after you summarize the plot of *American Beauty* (remember, you can't assume all your readers have seen the film—or that they remember it well if they have), you could offer the following specific examples as evidence:

The Burnham's home and neighborhood

Mrs. Burnham's obsession with appearance

The breakdown of the Burnham's marriage

Mr. Burnham's fantasies

Mr. Burnham's rebellion against the status quo

Mrs. Burnham's affair

The hatred Jane Burnham harbors for her parents

Mrs. Fitts' comatose state

Mr. Fitts' repressed homosexuality

Ricky Fitts' drug use and charade

Specific examples like these provide concrete evidence of your assertion. They make your claim "real" for your readers.

FACTS

Another form of evidence is facts, which are distinct from opinions:

A fact is:

   something known for certain to have happened
   something known for certain to be true
   something known for certain to exist

An opinion is:

   something believed to have happened
   something believed to be true
   something believed to exist

Facts are what we **know**; they are **objective** and therefore do not change from person to person. Opinions, on the other hand, are what we **believe**; they are **subjective** and debatable, and they often do change from person to person. Because facts are objective, they're particularly valuable as evidence in an essay, especially when your thesis is highly controversial.

Types of facts include statistics, definitions, recorded statements, and observations. For example, imagine you are drafting an essay in which you are assessing the flat tax (remember the outline from Lesson 6?). Here's your thesis:

A flat tax would be good for the government and for citizens.

To help support your thesis, you could include the following facts:

The IRS publishes 480 different tax forms.
The IRS publishes 280 different forms to explain those 480 tax forms.
The body of the tax law has 7.05 million words—ten times the number of words in the Bible.
The cost of income tax compliance is over $1.3 billion per year (some sources estimate the cost is as high as $2 billion).

> **A Note about Statistics.** Statistics may seem like the most incontestable kind of fact—after all, numbers are objective. But numbers *can* be, and often are, manipulated, and figures are often taken out of context. Alert readers will want to see the *source* of your statistics to be sure the figures are free from bias. (You'll learn more about this issue in the next lesson.)

PRACTICE 1

Choose one of the essays for which you developed an outline in Lesson 6 or 7. List at least four supporting ideas for your thesis. Include at least one specific example and at least one fact.

_____

_____

_____

_____

_____

REASONS

A third type of support is reasons. For many essays, the best way to support your thesis is to explain *why* you think what you do. Some reasons will be facts; others will be opinions. The key to this type of support is logic. Are your reasons logical? That is, are they based on evidence or good common sense?

In many cases, your reasons will require considerable support to demonstrate that they are logical. Take, for instance, the following thesis:

Animals should no longer be used in medical research.

You could offer the following reasons as support:

- *Medical research on animals is cruel.*
- *Medical research on animals is unnecessary.*

Both of these reasons are clearly opinions, and they need a good deal of support if your essay is to be convincing. Thus, you need to show your readers that these opinions are **reasonable** (logical). To support your assertion that medical research on animals is cruel, you could cite examples of some of the specific experiments conducted on animals (a combination of specific example, fact, and description); tell the story of a certain animal or experiment (specific example, anecdote); and provide expert opinion.

To support your assertion that medical research on animals is unnecessary, you could describe the technology that enables researchers to experiment on "virtual" humans; cite the fact that because of differences in physiology, results from research conducted on even our closest primate relatives can't be reliably translated into human terms; and cite expert opinion.

Of course, people's reasons for believing certain things are often very personal and highly debatable. While it's fine—and often even effective—to use emotional arguments to convince your readers, the more logical your reasons, the more effective they will be as support.

DESCRIPTIONS AND ANECDOTES

Evidence and support can also come in the form of descriptions and anecdotes. An anecdote is a brief description of an event, a very short story that helps to illustrate a point. Descriptions and anecdotes are effective evidence—especially in essays about people—because they help readers form pictures that illustrate your ideas. For example, imagine you make the following assertion for a college application essay:

> *The person I admire most is my sister. I call her the Bionic Woman. A single mother and a full-time professional, she is the strongest person I know.*

The best kind of support for this essay will come from description and anecdote—a series of "snapshots" and stories that illustrate your sister's strength. Here's an example:

> *Amy's divorce alone could have broken her. But she refused to let it. As usual, she took action. She sat down with her daughters and drew signs to post around the neighborhood. They hung the signs on telephone poles, in the post office, in the coffee shops around town. And within a few weeks, Amy was hosting her first divorced mothers group meeting. That was four years ago. Today she and her daughters are still close friends with the mothers and daughters who helped them through a difficult time.*

Similarly, to support your assertion that experiments on animals are cruel, you can describe an experiment in detail. Jean Bethke Elshtain, in her 1990 essay "Why Worry about the Animals?" (published in *The Progressive*), uses the following description to support her assertion that animals should not be used for any nonmedical research:

> *Most notorious of the "tests" deployed by the multibillion-dollar cosmetics industry is the Draize, which has been used since the 1940s to measure the potential irritative effects of products. Rabbits—used because their eyes do not produce tears and, therefore, cannot cleanse themselves—are placed into stocks and their eyes are filled with foreign substances. When a rabbit's eyes ulcerate—again, no pain killers are used—the cosmetic testers (who are usually not trained laboratory researchers) report a result.*

This is just one of many experiments Elshtain describes, and the result is a powerful, disturbing, and convincing essay.

EXPERT OPINION AND ANALYSIS

During a trial, lawyers will often call upon *expert witnesses* to help them make their case. These witnesses were not involved in the crime, but they have some expertise that can help the jurors determine the guilt or innocence of the defendant. Similarly, in many essays, and particularly in research papers, much of your support will come in the form of expert opinion and analysis. The experts you call upon can help you demonstrate the validity of your thesis.

You can collect expert opinion and analysis in two ways: by interviewing sources yourself (primary research), or by finding print or other recorded sources of expert opinion or analysis (secondary research). Secondary sources include periodicals, journals, books, and transcripts.

The strength of expert opinion and analysis as evidence comes from the fact that your sources *are experts*. They've spent a great deal of time studying the issue or experiencing the phenomenon you're describing. In most cases, they know the issue far better than you or your readers do.

Of course, quoting from an expert won't do you much good if you don't let your readers know that your source is an expert. Whether you're quoting, paraphrasing, or even just summarizing information from an expert, be sure to let your readers know the basis of your source's expertise. For example, in your essay about the flat tax, you might support your argument with the following expert sources and their opinions:

- *Dr. Alan Auerbach, professor of economics at the University of California of Berkeley and former chief economist at the Joint Committee on Taxation, estimates that the average family of four will have $3,000 more in income per year with a flat tax.*

- *The Tax Foundation, a nonprofit tax think tank, estimates that America spends $140 billion complying with the current tax code—a cost that would be reduced 94 percent by instituting a flat tax.*

In both cases, you've clearly identified your sources, both of which are obviously experts in the subject matter.

QUOTATIONS FROM THE TEXT

When you write about literature, much of your evidence will come from the text itself. For example, imagine that you've written the following thesis statement:

In his poem "Ad," Kenneth Fearing uses irony and structure to criticize the way governments recruit soldiers for war.

To support your assertion, you'll need to discuss the poem's content, structure, and style. But that's only half of the task. In addition to *telling* readers why you think what you do about the poem, you also need to *show* them the evidence that led you to your conclusion. Thus, you can *tell* readers that the poem is set up like a help-wanted ad and then show them proof by quoting the first and last lines of the poem: "*Wanted:* Men" and "Wages: *Death*." You can tell readers that Fearing suggests governments actively recruit men without morals, and then show them the evidence by quoting lines 6–8 of the poem:

If you thrill at the thought of throwing poison into wells,
have heavenly visions of people, by the thousands, dying in flames—
You are the very man we want.

PRACTICE 2

Provide support for another essay outlined in Lesson 6 or 7, or add more support to the essay you used for Practice 1 in this lesson. List four supporting ideas below, using at least two of the following types of evidence: reasons, descriptions or anecdotes, expert opinion and analysis, or quotations from the text.

_____

_____

_____

_____

_____

IN SHORT

Like lawyers in a courtroom trial, essay writers need to provide evidence for their assertions. That evidence can come in the form of specific examples, facts, reasons, descriptions and anecdotes, expert opinion and analysis, and quotations from the text.

Skill Building Until Next Time

Reread an essay that you believe is particularly effective. How does the author support his or her ideas? What kind of evidence does he or she provide? After you read this essay, keep it handy because you'll need to use it again in the next lesson.

L · E · S · S · O · N

STRATEGIES FOR CONVINCING

11

LESSON SUMMARY

While strong evidence is essential for an effective essay, it may not be enough to make your essay convincing. This lesson offers several strategies to help make your essays more persuasive.

B ecause most essays are about what you think and why you think so, most essays are really exercises in persuasive writing. You may want to persuade readers to change their point of view or to support a specific cause. But even when your primary goal isn't to persuade, you're still writing to convince. Because essays are built upon the assertion-support structure, your underlying goal is to convince readers that your thesis is valid.

Of course, the best way to convince readers that your thesis is valid is to provide strong and sufficient support. How you present your evidence, though, can often make or break your essay. The rest of this lesson presents seven strategies to help make your essays more convincing:

- be specific
- don't include ideas you can't support
- establish credibility
- acknowledge counterarguments
- make concessions
- avoid absolutes
- don't offend

BE SPECIFIC

Whatever your topic or assignment, the more specific you can be throughout your essay, the easier it will be for readers to accept your assertions. Specific examples and details help readers see what you're saying by making your abstract ideas concrete. The more concrete your ideas, the easier they will be for readers to accept.

For example, look at the difference between the two paragraphs below. The first lacks specific examples and details and therefore lacks persuasive power. The second paragraph, however, offers some very specific examples and details. It is therefore much more convincing:

To confirm my hypothesis, I asked my peers about the balance between work and play. Most of them said they thought the balance should be about equal. Several of them pointed out that because of technology, the distinction between work and home is fading, so it's especially important to set aside time to play.

To confirm my hypothesis, I interviewed 30 of my peers—students from both the public and private high schools in my area. I asked, "What do you think is the right relationship between work and play?" Twenty-two respondents said they think work and play should have equal time in our lives. "We should play at least as much as we work," said Ellen Reese, a senior planning to major in computer science. "Of course, that's a lot easier to do if you love your job, because then that's part of the play, too." Andrew Fry, a junior who wants to be a journalist, was one of twelve respondents concerned with the collapsing distinction between work and home. "Between e-mail, cell phones, and the Internet, we can take our work with us anywhere and work any time of the day. So many people bring their work home with them and let it eat up their playtime. I think it's really important to set aside time each day, or at least each week, to relax and play."

Notice how the writer of the second paragraph offers specific information: the number of students she polled, the kind of students she polled, and the exact question she asked them. This gives readers a much clearer sense of her survey and helps them better understand its results. Then, instead of generalizing the responses, she offers more specifics—like exactly how many students felt there should be an equal balance. Importantly, she also offers specific responses. She doesn't just *tell* us what people said; she *shows* us by quoting their responses. Once again, abstract ideas and generalizations are made more concrete—and therefore more convincing.

IF YOU CAN'T SUPPORT IT, DON'T INCLUDE IT

Imagine you are on a jury. The prosecuting attorney turns to the jury box and says, "The defendant is clearly guilty. I just know it." But he doesn't offer any evidence to back up his assertion. Absurd, of course. No legitimate lawyer would dream of making such a claim if he wasn't able to support it. This is a good policy for essay writers to abide by as well. As much as you may believe something to be true, as much as you may want to say something about your subject, if you can't provide evidence for that assertion, it doesn't belong in your essay.

For example, say you believe that Americans today work more hours and have less time for leisure than ever before. There are probably statistics out there to support this assertion, but you don't have time to find those sta-

tistics or gather expert opinion. As strongly as you may feel about this idea, since you can't support it, you shouldn't include it.

That doesn't mean you have to scrap the idea altogether, though. You don't have the time to find evidence for the claim that *Americans* in general work more and play less than ever before. But you *do* have evidence to support the assertion on a smaller scale. You can soften your assertion by reducing its scope and stating the following:

These days, everyone in my family is working more than ever—both at home and at the office.

If you can support *this* assertion with specific evidence—examples, facts, anecdotes, and so on—then it has a legitimate place in your essay.

ESTABLISH CREDIBILITY

Credibility is the quality of being trustworthy and believable. The more credible a person is, the more likely you are to accept his or her opinions as valid (well-founded, logical). As a writer, you need to establish credibility on two levels: your own credibility and the credibility of your sources.

Credibility is built upon two factors: **expertise** and freedom from **bias**. A *bias* is an opinion or feeling that strongly favors one side over others. *Expertise* is established by education, experience, jobs or position, reputation, and achievements. In general, the greater the expertise and the lower the potential for bias, the greater the credibility.

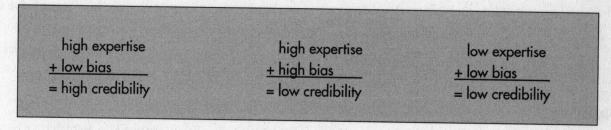

high expertise
+ low bias
= high credibility

high expertise
+ high bias
= low credibility

low expertise
+ low bias
= low credibility

THE CREDIBILITY OF YOUR SOURCES

As mentioned in Lesson 10, when you use expert opinion or analysis to support your assertions, it's important to let readers know who your sources are and how it is that they have expertise in the subject. Of course, you don't have room to include extensive biographies of each source. But you *do* have room to include some basic information to establish expertise. If your source is a person, include his or her title and perhaps a major achievement or two. If your source is an organization, let readers know a bit about the organization's history or achievements. For example, let's look again at the expert sources used for the flat tax essay:

- *Dr. Alan Auerbach, professor of economics at the University of California of Berkeley and former chief economist at the Joint Committee on Taxation, estimates that the average family of four will have $3000 more in income per year with a flat tax.*

- *The Tax Foundation, a nonprofit tax think tank, estimates that America spends $140 billion complying with the current tax code—a cost that would be reduced 94 percent by instituting a flat tax.*

In the first example, the writer tells readers Dr. Auerbach's current and former positions, both of which demonstrate that he is an expert in the subject matter. In the second example, the title of the organization—The Tax Foundation—tells readers that the organization is devoted to the issue of taxes. The writer describes it as a "think tank," which suggests that it seeks out and employs experts in the subject matter.

These sources, then, have expertise. But that doesn't mean they're credible. The most knowledgeable sources may also be the most biased. In order for your sources to be perceived as trustworthy, you need to demonstrate that they are free of bias. What if, for example, Dr. Auerbach was also an advisor to the Republican Flat Tax Committee? If so, he probably has a vested interest in acceptance of the flat tax proposal. And because numbers can be manipulated (especially numbers of this sort, since budgeting formulas can vary greatly), readers should be careful about accepting his opinion.

On the other hand, if Dr. Auerbach were a Democrat (which he is), readers would have more reason to believe that he is unbiased, since the flat tax is a Republican proposal that has received little Democratic support. Auerbach's party affiliation can easily be added to the sentence to improve his credibility.

YOUR OWN CREDIBILITY

The best way to establish your expertise is to demonstrate to readers that you've "done your homework"—that is, that you've considered the issues carefully and conducted the research, if necessary, to support your position. To show readers that you are not unfairly biased, you'll also need to acknowledge counterarguments and make concessions. These two strategies are explained in the sections that follow.

PRACTICE 1

Imagine you're writing an essay about the impact of violence on television. Below are two facts (which have been made up for the purpose of this exercise) and their sources. Create a brief profile of each source to make that source credible. Then, for each fact, write a sentence that includes the fact, its source, and enough information about the source to establish its credibility.

Fact 1: The average television channel shows 579 acts of violence in a 24-hour period.
Source: Emily Rhodes
Profile:

_____

_____

_____

Sentence:

_____

Fact 2:   Violent crimes committed by juveniles have quadrupled since 1973.
Source: Children's Watch.
Profile:

_____

_____

_____

Sentence:

_____

ACKNOWLEDGE COUNTERARGUMENTS

One of the keys to establishing your credibility and persuading readers is acknowledging counterarguments. Counterarguments are those arguments that might be offered by someone supporting the other side. That is, if you are arguing that "medical research on animals is unnecessary," you need to consider what someone arguing that "medical research on animals is necessary" would think.

Acknowledging counterarguments strengthens your argument. For one thing, it shows that you have considered all sides of the issue and thought carefully about the logic of your position. More importantly, it helps you better defend your position. If you know what objections your readers will have, then you can systematically address those objections in your essay. Furthermore, acknowledging counterarguments enables you to win your readers over by addressing their concerns and then countering each concern with a reasonable premise of your own.

For example, compare the two arguments below:

Lukas, can I borrow your car tomorrow morning? I have a job interview and I can't get there by bus. I really want this job. What do you say?

Lukas, I know you don't like to let other people drive your car, especially since you put so much time into rebuilding it. But I'm hoping you'll make an exception. I have a job interview tomorrow and I can't get there by bus. I'm really excited about this job. I promise to have it back by noon with a full tank of gas. And to show my appreciation, I'll take her to the car wash on my way back.

It's clear that the speaker in the second paragraph took some time to consider Lukas's point of view. By addressing Lukas's concerns, the writer shows Lukas that he's put himself in Lukas's shoes, and this kind of empathy can go a long way when you're trying to convince readers.

One way to help you acknowledge counterarguments is to play "devil's advocate." Take a few moments to imagine that you are writing an essay with the opposite thesis. Doing so will help you anticipate what the other side will say, so you can acknowledge those arguments and come up with effective counter-arguments. It will also help you find holes in your argument that you didn't realize you had.

Acknowledging counterarguments is not the same as *supporting* them. In fact, if you acknowledge counter-arguments strategically, you can actually use them to help support your case. For example, imagine you are arguing that uniforms should be mandatory for all public school students. One of your major supporting ideas is that school uniforms will create a stronger sense of community. After playing devil's advocate, you realize that people against this idea would argue that school uniforms create a culture of conformity. Here's how you might acknowledge the counterargument, show its weakness, and set the reader up for your position:

> *Many people have argued that school uniforms would encourage* conformity, *and that schools should do all that they can to help students develop a sense of individuality. But as much as we want to believe that the way we dress is an expression of our individuality, for most students, clothing is more often a means of conformity. Students want to dress like their peers.* They want to wear the same brands and the same styles as their friends (or the people whom they wish were their friends). It is the rare student who truly uses clothing as an expression of individuality.*

Now that the writer has addressed the counter argument, he can go on to develop his position—that school uniforms will create a sense of community.

PRACTICE 2

You are writing an essay on the subject of censorship on the Internet. Take a stance on this issue and write a brief thesis statement on a separate sheet of paper or your computer. Then, come up with three supporting points. Next, play devil's advocate and list three points the opposition might make. Finally, write a brief paragraph in which you acknowledge one of those points.

MAKE CONCESSIONS

As important as acknowledging the opposition is acknowledging the holes in your argument. Admitting your argument's flaws makes more sense than you might think. By admitting your argument's flaws, you show your readers that you've really thought your argument through. It also shows that you are not so blinded by your opinions that you can't see problems (or potential problems) with your position. In short, it shows that you have used **logic** as well as emotion in considering your argument. Finally, it also strengthens your argument by showing that despite its weaknesses, you still support your position.

To show how this works, let's return to the issue of the flat tax. Instituting a flat tax would mean a drastic restructuring of the tax system. Because the flat tax is much simpler than our current system, it would require far less oversight and use far fewer resources—which means that thousands of IRS employees would lose their

jobs. This is an unavoidable effect of instituting a flat tax, and it's a point that you might have difficulty countering. Instead, you should concede that this is a painful but necessary step to fixing the tax system.

Here is how you might concede that point:

> *Of course, a flat tax would dramatically streamline the tax filing, collecting, and reviewing processes—and that means the IRS, the nation's largest government agency, would have to be considerably downsized. Indeed, a flat tax would probably mean thousands of IRS employees would lose their jobs. Unfortunately, this is a price we must pay if we want to end the billions of dollars we waste each year with the current bloated tax system.*

This writer doesn't offer a counterargument. Instead, she acknowledges the problems as an inevitable part of a flat tax reform.

Avoid Absolutes

As much as people would like things to be black and white, the reality is that the world is filled with shades of gray. That's why people run into trouble when they phrase things in absolute terms. There is always an exception, and a good essay will be careful to avoid statements that don't allow for those exceptions. Most absolutes are gross generalizations or stereotypes anyway—two things you want to avoid in an essay.

Failure to acknowledge exceptions will seriously undermine your credibility with your reader, especially if your reader happens to be one of those exceptions. For example, imagine you state the following in your essay:

> *Little Red Riding Hood is portrayed as naïve and innocent, just like all girls in fairy tales.*

Well, maybe in all the fairy tales *you've* read—but in fact many fairy tales describe girls who are sophisticated, cunning and even, in some cases, dangerous. There are many exceptions to the "rule" you've just established, and thoughtful readers will be frustrated by such a statement.

To allow for exceptions, soften your "absolutes." The addition of a single word like "many" or "most" can change a problematic, implausible absolute into a plausible, provable statement. Here are some phrases to help you avoid absolutes:

Instead of "all," say:	Instead of "none," say:
most	almost none
many	very few
just about all/just about every	with few exceptions
nearly all	only a handful
the majority of	
some	

Thus, you could revise your fairy tale statement as follows:

> *Little Red Riding Hood is portrayed as naïve and innocent, like many girls in fairy tales.*

DON'T OFFEND

Lastly, if you want to convince readers, don't offend them. Students often don't realize that something they've written may offend readers—but that's usually because they have a very specific reader in mind. That is, they imagine a general reader who has a lot more in common with them than a true general reader might. This enables students to write a statement like:

Creationists are simply unable to distinguish between fact and opinion.

Besides being an absolute statement (suggesting that *all* creationists fit this bill), this claim is just plain insulting to creationists. You may think that creationism is bunk—but a lot of people (including some very highly regarded scientists) do not. If your reader happens to be a creationist, however strong your arguments were to this point, you've probably lost his support now. Even if your readers aren't creationists, they're likely to bristle at your insensitivity, and as a result you'll lose credibility in their eyes as well.

IN SHORT

Writers use several different strategies to make their essays more convincing. They provide specific detail to make ideas more concrete; they establish credibility, acknowledge counterarguments, and make concessions; they don't include assertions they can't support; they avoid absolutes; and they take care not to offend their readers.

Skill Building Until Next Time

Take another look at the essay that you read for the Skill Building Until Next Time segment in Lesson 10. What strategies for convincing do you see at work? Does the essay include lots of specific detail? Does the writer establish credibility? How? Does he or she acknowledge counterarguments? Make concessions? How?

L·E·S·S·O·N

INTRODUCTIONS

12

LESSON SUMMARY

First impressions are important. This lesson explains the purpose of introductions and how to write an introduction that grabs your reader's attention.

Right or wrong, in the business world, many decisions are made based solely on first impressions. Companies spend thousands—even millions—in advertising dollars to make sure your first impression of them is a good one.

First impressions are just as important in writing. After all, writing, too, is an exchange of "goods"—the writer's ideas for the reader's time. And readers often decide whether or not to invest their precious time based solely on the introduction.

WHAT AN INTRODUCTION SHOULD DO

The introduction is a distinct part of the essay because it serves a distinct function. A combination of simple courtesy and strategy, the introduction acquaints readers with the subject and purpose of the essay. If done well, an introduction will also compel the reader to read the rest of the essay.

Specifically, essay writers have four tasks to accomplish within the first few paragraphs. An effective introduction should do the following four tasks.

1. **Provide the context necessary to understand your thesis.** Remember, in most cases, you're writing for a *general audience.* That means readers don't know who you are. They don't know your assignment. And they may not be familiar with the issues or texts you are discussing. Thus, you may need to provide some basic background information. For example, if you are writing about literature, you should include the titles, authors, and publication dates of the texts you will be analyzing. Similarly, if you are writing about a historical event, you should name the event, the date, and the key people (or countries, or issues, and so on) involved. Here's an example:

   Mary Shelley's novel Frankenstein *was published over 180 years ago. But this remarkable novel raises a question that is more important today than ever: What is a creator's responsibility for his or her creation?*

2. **Clearly state the main point of the essay.** Your readers should know from the beginning what idea you will be developing throughout the essay. A clear thesis statement is a key component of an effective introduction. (See Lesson 9 for a review of thesis statements.)

   In the example above, the last sentence expresses the main idea of the essay—that the question of responsibility is more important today than ever.

3. **Set the tone for the essay.** Like the opening notes of a song give you a sense of the listening experience ahead, an introduction gives readers a sense of what they're going to experience by setting the tone of the essay. Tone is the mood or attitude conveyed through language, particularly through word choice and sentence structure. Your tone may be personal and informal, serious and formal, urgent, relaxed, grave, or humorous. In the example above, the language is very straightforward, rather on the serious and formal side. This is fitting, as the subject is a serious one and the supporting examples include such serious matters as atomic weapons and cloning.

4. **Grab the reader's interest.** Consider all of the things that compete for your reader's attention. To get readers to devote time to your essay, you must grab their attention. This means you need an introduction that stands out—one that piques their interest and makes them want to learn more. This is one thing that the introduction above does *not* do well—a problem you'll see corrected in one of the examples below.

WAYS TO GRAB YOUR READER'S INTEREST

There are many different strategies writers use to create eye-catching introductions. What these strategies have in common is an element of creativity and an awareness of the reader's needs. They do not simply announce the subject or the thesis; they do not make huge generalizations that sound grand but leave the reader feeling empty. (Here's an example: "For thousands of years, humans have been trying to figure out the key to happiness." Big statement. Small impact.)

The seven introductory strategies below offer specific ways to get into your subject and thesis that naturally arouse a reader's attention. They make your introduction an *invitation* to read more. These strategies are:

- a quotation
- a question
- a surprising statement or fact
- an imaginary situation or scenario
- an anecdote
- interesting background information
- a new twist on a familiar phrase

A QUOTATION

Start off with a quotation—from a text, a film, a subject-matter expert—heck, even your grandmother, if she happens to have said something relevant to the topic and interesting to your reader. Here's an example:

> *"All animals are equal, but some animals are more equal than others," said Napoleon in George Orwell's classic novel* Animal Farm. *Uncle Sam might say something similar: "All people must pay taxes, but some must pay more taxes than others." Our current federal income tax system treats taxpayers unfairly and requires a monumental budget to administer and maintain. A flat tax, which would treat all tax payers equally and dramatically reduce tax compliance cost, is the answer.*

A QUESTION

Open up with a question to get your readers thinking. Of course, the question (and its answer) should be relevant to your thesis. Here's an example:

> *What's in a name? Nothing—and everything. It is, after all, just a name, one tiny piece of the puzzle that is you. But when you have a nickname like "Dumbo," a name can become the major force in shaping your sense of who you are. That's how it was for me.*

A SURPRISING STATEMENT OR FACT

Begin your essay with a surprising statement or fact. This kind of introduction grabs readers' attention with its "shock value." Here's an example:

> *If you don't believe our current tax law is ridiculously out of control, just consider this: our total tax law consists of 101,295 pages and 7.05 million words. That means our tax law has almost 100 times more pages and ten times as many words as the Bible. Bloated? You bet. But it doesn't have to be. The government would earn equal or greater tax revenue and save millions of dollars in compliance costs by instituting a flat tax system.*

PRACTICE 1

On a separate sheet of paper or your computer, write an introduction for one of the essays you brainstormed or outlined or for one of the examples provided in the first half of this book. Use one of these strategies: a quotation, a question, or a surprising statement or fact.

AN IMAGINARY SITUATION OR SCENARIO

Hook your readers by creating an imaginary situation or describing a scenario. You can ask readers to place themselves in the scene, or you can have them witness it. Here's an example:

You've been drifting at sea for days with no food and no water. You have two companions. Suddenly a half-empty bottle of water floats by. You fight over the bottle ready to kill the others if you have to for that water. What has happened? What are you—human or animal? It is a question that H. G. Wells raises over and over in The Island of Dr. Moreau. *His answer? Like it or not, we're both.*

AN ANECDOTE

Start your essay with an anecdote. Tell a short, interesting story related to your subject or thesis. Here's an example:

I'd been getting into a lot of trouble—failing classes, starting fights, taking things that didn't belong to me. So the guidance counselor at school suggested that my folks take me to a psychiatrist. "You mean a shrink?!" my mother replied, horrified. My father and I had the same reaction. After all, what good would it do to lie on a couch while some "doctor" asked questions and took notes? So I went to my first session angry and skeptical. But after a few weeks, I realized that we had it all wrong. Those "shrinks" really know what they're doing. And mine helped me turn my life around.

INTERESTING BACKGROUND INFORMATION

Begin by offering some interesting background information about the topic. Here's a revision of the *Frankenstein* introduction using this strategy:

Incredibly, Frankenstein—*one of the most important novels in western literature—was written by a teenager. When it was published in 1818, Mary Shelley was only 19 years old. Despite her youth, Shelley's story raises a question that is more important to us today than ever: What is the creator's relationship to his or her creation?*

A NEW TWIST ON A FAMILIAR PHRASE

Finally, try opening your essay with a new twist on a familiar phrase. Here's an example:

To eat or not to eat? That is the question millions of Americans struggle with every day as they fight the battle of the bulge. But it seems to be a losing battle. Despite the millions spent on diet pills and diet plans, Americans today are heavier than ever.

There are lots of reasons for this nationwide weight gain, but experts agree that the main cause is lack of exercise. And one of the main reasons we don't get enough exercise is because we spend too much time in front of the TV.

Notice that this introduction is actually two paragraphs. And that's quite all right. For some essays, a three or four paragraph introduction is appropriate. The key is to have an introduction that is in the right proportion to the rest of the essay. If your essay is only two pages long, then one paragraph should be sufficient for your introduction. Otherwise, you risk tipping the delicate balance between the introduction and body of the essay. On the other hand, if your essay is ten or twelve pages long, then it may take you a couple of solid paragraphs to properly introduce your topic and thesis. You might have a more detailed anecdote, for example, or spend two or three paragraphs describing a scenario that sets up your thesis.

PRACTICE 2

Write a two to three paragraph introduction for one of the essays you brainstormed or outlined or for one of the examples provided in the first half of this book. Use one of the strategies described in the second half of this lesson: an imaginary situation or scenario, an anecdote, interesting background information, or a new twist on a familiar phrase.

In Short

Introductions serve an important function. They "welcome" your reader into your essay by providing context, stating your thesis, and setting the tone. They should also grab your reader's interest. Strategies for attention-grabbing openers include starting with a quotation, a question, a surprising statement or fact, an imaginary situation or scenario, an anecdote, interesting background information, or a new twist on a familiar phrase.

Skill Building Until Next Time

Page through a magazine, reading only the introductions to the articles. What techniques do writers use to grab your interest? Do the introductions provide context and state the main point of the article? What tone do they set for the rest of the essay?

L · E · S · S · O · N
CONCLUSIONS
13

LESSON SUMMARY

How you conclude your essay is just as important as how you introduce it. This lesson will explain what conclusions should do and how to write an ending with impact.

Have you ever been enjoying a movie only to find yourself disappointed by how it ends? Though the ending may be just a small fraction of the movie's length, if it's not satisfying, it can ruin the whole experience. The same is often true of essays. A powerful conclusion can dramatically improve a reader's impression of a weak or mediocre essay, while a weak conclusion can do the reverse, leaving a bad impression of an otherwise well-written essay.

WHAT A CONCLUSION SHOULD DO

Like the introduction, the conclusion of an essay serves a specific function. Its job is to wrap things up in a way that makes readers feel satisfied with their reading experience. Writers create this sense of satisfaction in four ways:

1. by restating the thesis

2. by offering a new understanding

3. by providing a sense of closure

4. by arousing readers' emotions

RESTATING THE THESIS

Before you say good-bye to your readers, it's a good idea to remind them of what you wanted them to get from your essay. Reminding readers of your thesis will help ensure that they get, and remember, your main point. This doesn't mean you should restate your thesis in exactly the same words, however. In fact, you should avoid this approach, especially in shorter essays. Instead, *rephrase* your thesis. You said it at the beginning; you presented your support; now it's time to remind readers what idea you were supporting, but in a new way.

Readers need to feel like the essay has taken them somewhere. Repeating the exact same sentence (or even key phrases) may make readers feel like they're back at the beginning—or like you just can't come up with anything else to say. Rephrasing your thesis refocuses readers on your central idea without unnecessary repetition. Here's an example of how one writer restated his thesis:

Introduction: *What's in a name? Nothing—and everything. It is, after all, just a name, one tiny piece of the puzzle that is you. But when you have a nickname like "Dumbo," a name can become a major force in shaping your sense of who you are. That's how it was for me.*

Conclusion: *I don't blame my brother for how I turned out, of course. He may have given me the nickname, but I'm the one who let that nickname determine how I felt about myself. I could have worn the name proudly— after all, Disney's Dumbo is a hero. Instead, I wore it like a dunce cap. I wish I had known then what I know now: that you are what you believe yourself to be.*

OFFERING A NEW UNDERSTANDING

To conclude means *to bring to an end*. But it also means *to arrive at a belief or opinion by reasoning*. And that's what a good conclusion should do: It should both bring the essay to an end *and* end with a conclusion—the understanding that you have come to by working through your essay. After all, you stated a thesis and then supported it with evidence. That has to add up to something. You should now have a deeper understanding of your subject, and it's this understanding that you need to convey to your readers in your conclusion. This understanding makes readers feel as if their time has been well spent; it is their "reward" for reading your essay.

The word *conclude* means:
1. to bring to an end
2. to arrive at a belief or opinion by reasoning

In the example above, the writer offers a new understanding of how names can shape people. Readers learn that he had the choice to let the nickname shape him in a positive or negative way. This understanding is his "gift" to readers, and he shares it in his conclusion.

PROVIDING A SENSE OF CLOSURE

One of the most frustrating things a conclusion can do is to take the reader off in a new direction. Your conclusion should offer a new understanding, yes; but that understanding must be very closely related to the subject and thesis. In fact, it should really be an extension of your thesis. If you open up a new can of worms, so to speak, your readers will not only lose sight of your thesis, but they'll also feel frustrated. Instead of pulling everything together, you leave your essay full of loose threads. For example, look at the difference in the two conclusions below. The first, which you've already seen, provides a good sense of closure; the second, however, starts off in a new direction.

Closure:

I don't blame my brother for how I turned out, of course. He may have given me the nickname, but I'm the one who let that nickname determine how I felt about myself. I could have worn the name proudly—after all, Disney's Dumbo is a hero. Instead, I wore it like a dunce cap. I wish I had known then what I know now: that you are what you believe yourself to be.

Lacks Closure:

I don't blame my brother for how I turned out, of course. He may have given me the nickname, but I'm the one who let that nickname determine how I felt about myself. I could have worn the name proudly—after all, Disney's Dumbo is a hero. Disney knew what he was doing when he created the Dumbo character—he's someone most of us can relate to, and he has a lot to teach children.

Even though you don't know what is in the body of the essay, you can sense that the second conclusion lacks closure. It doesn't end with an idea related to the thesis; instead, it leads readers off in another direction. It leaves readers thinking about the movie *Dumbo*, not the writer's struggle with his nickname. Further, this conclusion ends by making a couple of assertions that have not been supported anywhere in the essay. Of course, since it's the end of the essay, there's no support for those ideas coming up ahead either.

THE ART OF FRAMING

One of the most effective ways to provide a sense of closure is to "frame" your essay with a conclusion that refers back to the introduction. That is, as you restate your thesis, use the same approach you used in your introduction. The idea isn't to *repeat* your introduction but rather to *remind* readers where they began their journey. This kind of reminder helps readers feel like they've come full circle—like they've gone from point A to point B and made all of the appropriate stops in between.

In the sample conclusions offered later in this lesson, notice how the "anecdote" conclusion frames the Dumbo essay by repeating the opening question and providing a more sophisticated answer. Similarly, the "call to action" conclusion frames the "To eat or not to eat?" essay by referring back to the essay's opening lines.

AROUSING THE READER'S EMOTIONS

Finally, a good conclusion should also *move* readers by arousing their emotions. Because your conclusion restates and extends your thesis by offering a new understanding—because you've taken the reader on a journey through your thoughts and experiences—and because, in the end, you want your essay to have impact—it's important to have an ending that's memorable. The way to make it memorable is to make it emotional. The conclusion to the Dumbo essay, for example, touches our emotions by making us think about how we may have let negative beliefs about ourselves dictate who we have become. At the same time, it inspires us by suggesting that we have the power to change ourselves if we have a negative self-image.

STRATEGIES FOR CONCLUSIONS

Just as there are many strategies for creating an attention-getting introduction, there are also many ways to create a powerful conclusion. These six are among the most effective:

- a quotation
- a question
- an anecdote
- a prediction
- a solution or recommendation
- a call to action

A QUOTATION

Three of the strategies for introducing an essay are also effective strategies for conclusions: quotations, questions, and anecdotes. Here's how you might use a quotation to sum up an essay:

In Grand Illusion, *the whole idea of nationhood is exposed as an illusion, and the fact that we go to war over an illusion is the film's great irony—and tragedy. It is a tragedy Renoir hopes we can avoid repeating. If "losing an illusion makes you wiser than finding a truth," as Ludwig Borne wrote, then Renoir has succeeded in making us all so much wiser.*

A QUESTION

Here's how you might use a question to conclude an essay:

"What kind of place is America?" you asked. In short, America is an idea and an experiment. We call the idea "democracy," and we see what happens when we let people say whatever they want, go wherever they want, and, in most cases, do whatever they want. True, the results aren't always pretty. But it certainly is a beautiful experiment, isn't it?

AN ANECDOTE

Anecdotes make for good conclusions, too. Here's an example. Notice how it frames the essay by repeating the question used in the introduction:

Introduction: What's in a name? Nothing—and everything. It is, after all, just a name, one tiny piece of the puzzle that is you. But when you have a nickname like "Dumbo," a name can become the major force in shaping your sense of who you are. That's how it was for me.

Conclusion: What's in a name? Enough to make me think long and hard about what to name my son before he was born. I spent months researching names and their meanings and thinking about the nicknames people might come up with. Once we finally settled on a name, I spent many sleepless nights worrying that we'd made the wrong choice and petrified that Samuel James would hate us for giving him that name. But I've realized that along the way, Sam will have to learn the same lesson I did. I only hope that I can help make it less painful.

PRACTICE 1

On a separate sheet of paper or your computer, write a conclusion for one of the essays you brainstormed or outlined or for one of the examples provided in the first half of this book. Use one of the strategies described so far in this lesson: a quotation, a question, or an anecdote. If possible, use one of the same topics for which you wrote an introduction in Lesson 12 so that you can frame the essay.

A PREDICTION

You can close your essay with a prediction about the future of a person, place, or thing related to your thesis. Here's an example from an "about us" college application essay:

Twenty years from now, when I'm 47, I will retire and survey my empire. I will have created and led a hugely successful Fortune 500 company; I will have used my considerable wealth to set up a literacy foundation and establish scholarships for needy children; and I will have set up a home for orphaned children in my native country. Deeply satisfied with my accomplishments, I will then make a generous gift to Briarwood College, for I will recall with great gratitude that my education there made all of my accomplishments possible.

A SOLUTION OR RECOMMENDATION

Conclude with a solution to the problem you've been discussing or a recommendation for future action. Here's an example from an essay that examines misinformation on the Internet:

While the Internet can be a very valuable source of information, it contains so much misinformation that it's almost criminal. Though we can't—and shouldn't—regulate what people put up on the Web, we can—and should—provide guidance for citizens surfing the Web. Why not create a "reliability index" that measures the trustworthiness of Web sites? Then the Web can truly be what it was meant to be: an asset, not a liability.

A CALL TO ACTION

Finally, you can end an essay by suggesting a specific action that your readers should take. Here's an example of a conclusion for the essay about television and lack of exercise. Notice how it frames the essay by referring back to the opening line of the introduction:

Introduction: To eat or not to eat? That is the question millions of Americans struggle with every day as they fight the battle of the bulge. But it seems to be a losing battle. Despite the millions spent on diet pills and diet plans, Americans today are heavier than ever.

There are lots of reasons for this nationwide weight gain, but experts agree that the main cause is lack of exercise. And one of the main reasons we don't get enough exercise is because we spend too much time in front of the TV.

Conclusion: Television entertains and informs us. But it also fattens us. If you are one of the millions of Americans who are overweight, take a simple step toward a healthier body. Get up and turn off the tube. The question isn't "to eat or not to eat." Rather, the question is, what can you do instead of watching TV? Go for a walk. Take a swim. Ride a bike. Get some exercise! You'll end up with a much healthier body—and mind.

PRACTICE 2

On a separate sheet of paper or your computer, write a conclusion for one of the essays you brainstormed or outlined or for one of the examples provided in the first half of this book. This time, use one of the strategies described in the second half of this lesson: a prediction, a solution or recommendation, or a call to action. Again, if possible, use one of the same topics for which you wrote an introduction in Lesson 12 so that you can frame the essay.

IN SHORT

Like introductions, conclusions serve several important functions. They refocus the essay by restating the thesis; they offer a "gift" to the reader in the form of a new understanding, an extension of that thesis; they provide a sense of closure; and they arouse readers' emotions. Some of the same strategies for introductions also work well for conclusions, including quotations, questions, and anecdotes. Other closing techniques include a prediction, a solution or recommendation, and a call to action.

Skill Building Until Next Time

Page through a magazine, this time reading the introductions *and* conclusions to several articles. What techniques do writers use to conclude their articles? Do the conclusions restate the main idea offered in the introduction? Do they go a step further and offer a new idea? Do they provide a sense of closure? Do they arouse your emotions? What techniques do the writers use to conclude their articles?

S·E·C·T·I·O·N 3

REVISING AND EDITING

Once you have a draft, the next step is to revise and edit your essay, reworking it to make sure it does what you intended it to do—and does it well. The lessons in this section will guide you through the revising and editing processes, showing you how to work from "big picture" issues like thesis and support down to the nitty-gritty details of grammar.

L·E·S·S·O·N 14

REVISING THE BIG PICTURE

LESSON SUMMARY

This lesson explains the revising process and shows you how to revise for three important "big picture" issues: fulfilling the assignment, stating a clear thesis, and providing strong support.

magine you've just completed a three-page draft of an essay. What should you do next?

A. Check for fragments and run-on sentences.
B. Correct all of the spelling mistakes.
C. Make sure you have commas in all the right places.
D. None of the above.

The best answer is D—none of the above. Although you've already completed two major steps in the writing process (planning and drafting), there is still one major step to go: revising. And *revising* should generally take place before you even think about the final step: *editing*.

UNDERSTANDING THE REVISING PROCESS

The word *revise* comes from the prefix *re*, meaning "again," and the French root *visere*, meaning "to examine." To revise means to examine (or

re-examine) and improve or amend; to (re)consider and then alter. In other words, it means carefully rereading your essay draft and then changing it to make it better.

The difference between **revising** and **editing** is important. Revision deals with the *content* and *style* of your essay—*what* you say and *how* you say it. It's about your ideas and how you organize and present them. Editing, on the other hand, deals with *grammar* (correct sentences), *mechanics* (correct spelling, capitalization, and punctuation), and *format* (correct arrangement on the page). Editing, of course, is very important; your writing should be as clean and error-free as possible. But it doesn't make much sense to carefully proofread every sentence only to realize that you need to cut three paragraphs and add two new ones to your essay. As a general rule, wait until you're confident that your essay says what you want it to say before you worry about editing.

> **Revising**: improving the content and style of your essay
> **Editing**: correcting the grammar, mechanics, and format of your essay

Revision actually takes place on three levels: on the "big picture" or essay level, on the paragraph level, and on the sentence level. It is recommended that you revise for the big picture first, then look at your paragraphs, and then focus on your sentences. Of course, you may not actually revise on each of these levels independently. You might, for example, revise sentences as you re-arrange paragraphs—and that's fine. But don't get too caught up in revising sentences before you've addressed the big picture issues. You might end up revising sentences only to delete them later because they don't really belong in your essay.

GETTING FEEDBACK

If you think professional writers work alone, think again. They know how important it is to get feedback before they send their work out into the world, and getting feedback is an integral part of their writing process.

As scary as it may be to show your draft to others, it is one of the best things you can do to improve your writing. Getting feedback can help you pinpoint your essay's strengths and weaknesses. You can learn what works well, and what doesn't; what comes across clearly to your readers, and what confuses them. Find someone you trust (or better yet, two or three people) to read and respond to your essay. Ask them to read carefully and answer the following questions:

- What do you like about my essay?
- Is there anything that seems confusing or unclear?
- Is there anything you need to know more about?
- What do you think I could do to improve this essay?

Listen carefully to your reader's feedback. It's often difficult to accept criticism about writing, and critics aren't always right. But chances are if a reader doesn't understand what you've written, or sees a purpose that's different from what you intended, then you probably need to revise.

READING OUT LOUD

If you don't have someone who can give you feedback—or even if you do—try reading your essay aloud. Read loudly and clearly, as if you are reading to an audience. As you read, *listen* to how your words sound. *Hear* what you've written.

Sometimes when people read silently, they automatically insert words that aren't actually there, or skim over something that seems clear, but isn't. However, when you read out loud, you can often hear where your wording sounds awkward or where your sentences are too long or confusing. You can also hear where your writing simply does not convey what it should or what you intended.

Reading out loud also helps you get used to your writing "voice"—how you sound on paper. If you read something out loud and it doesn't "sound like you," then you should revise it. Even straightforward subject test essays should have a personality—yours. And if it sounds false to you, it will probably sound false to your readers, too.

ALLOWING SUFFICIENT TIME FOR REVISING

Don't expect to draft an essay and revise it to a fine polish in one afternoon. Revising takes time. As you read through your draft, you might realize that you have to do more research, or you might decide that you want to draft several new paragraphs. You might feel that your essay would work better with a different organization (say, changing from most-to-least to least-to-most important), or you might decide that you need a great deal more variety in your sentence structure. All of this requires time.

Furthermore, revising is usually much more productive after you've distanced yourself a little bit from your draft. Let it sit for a couple of hours or a day or two if possible. Give it a good rest for 15 minutes at least while you think about something else. When you come back to your essay, you should be able to think more clearly and objectively about what you've written, and the distance you established will help you be more creative. Importantly, this distance will also make it easier for you to add and delete text throughout your essay.

LEARNING TO LET GO

Letting go of text that you've written is one of the hardest things about revising. Especially if writing doesn't come easily to you, you may be reluctant to change or eliminate sentences or paragraphs from your draft. Perhaps it will help to remember that even the best of the best don't get it right the first time. They write, and rewrite, and rewrite, and they spend more time crossing things out than they do anything else. Ernest Hemingway, for example, revised the last page of *A Farewell to Arms* 37 times. No college admissions officer or instructor expects you to revise an essay 37 times, of course. The point is this: Revising is about keeping what works in your essay and fixing what doesn't. And sometimes "fixing" means eliminating—even if it's one of the most beautiful paragraphs you've ever written. Hold on to it; it may come in handy in another essay sometime. But for now, it's best left unsaid.

LOOKING AT THE BIG PICTURE

Begin revising by looking at the two things that affect the whole essay: your thesis and its support. There are three questions to consider:

1. Have you fulfilled the requirements of the assignment?

2. Do you have one clear main idea?

3. Have you effectively supported that idea?

If the answer to any of these questions is "no," then you have some rewriting to do.

FULFILLING THE ASSIGNMENT

Of course, if your draft does not fulfill the requirements of the assignment, you need to find out where you went amiss and revise your essay until it does. This may mean changing your focus, or dealing with your topic in a different way (for example, maybe your essay *summarizes*, but the assignment asks you to *evaluate*.)

The first step, then, should be to review the assignment carefully. What subject or subjects are you supposed to address in your essay? Did you address them? Second, *how* are you supposed to address those subjects? Did you address them in that way?

Be sure you have a clear understanding of what exactly is expected of you before you begin to revise. Otherwise, you might revise in such a way that you end up with an essay that doesn't fulfill the assignment.

REVISING YOUR THESIS

Next, check to see whether or not your essay has one clear main idea. If it does, you (and any readers who give you feedback on your draft) should be able to readily identify it. It should be stated clearly in your thesis statement, and meet the requirements of the assignment. If your thesis is not clear, then you probably have one of these common problems:

- No thesis. Your essay may have a lot to say, but its paragraphs are not held together by one controlling idea. This type of essay is often the result of insufficient planning. If you took the time to consider your audience and purpose, brainstorm, and develop a tentative thesis and outline, then you should be able to avoid this problem.

- Your thesis is not what your essay supports. You do have a thesis, but the body of your essay actually supports a *different* idea. This often happens when writers discover, through the drafting process, that they feel differently about their topic than they originally thought. As a result, they end up building a case for a different thesis. If your essay does indeed support an idea that's different from your thesis, you have two choices: You can rewrite the *body* of the essay so that it supports the thesis, or you can revise your *thesis* so that it fits the body of the essay.

- More than one main idea. Your essay has not one main idea, but two—or even three. Perhaps during the planning stage you didn't sufficiently narrow your thesis. Or, as you researched, brainstormed, and drafted,

you found several ideas you wanted to explore. As a result, you have two or three underdeveloped mini essays rather than one fully developed idea. If you have more than one main idea, see if there is a way to tie your two main ideas together. Otherwise, you should choose the better of the two (or three) ideas and revise your essay to develop that idea alone.

GLOSSING

Each of the problems discussed above (and several others, as you'll see in a moment) can be discovered by a technique called *glossing*. Glossing is simply a way of outlining the ideas that are in your draft.

To gloss, read each paragraph in your draft carefully. Then, in the margin next to each paragraph, briefly note the following:

1. what the paragraph *is about* (its idea)

2. what the paragraph *does* (its function)

Here's an example of a student's essay that she glossed:

Paragraph	Idea	Function
When was the last time you told a lie? If you're like most people, it was probably pretty recently. Did you know that you can also lie without even saying a word? This kind of lie can be even more devastating.	Silent lies can be worse than regular lies	• Introduces essay • States thesis— ("This kind of lie…")
The poet Adrienne Rich said that "Lying is done with words and also with silence." "To lie" means "to tell something that is untrue." But it also means "to be deceptive." We often use silence to deceive. Rich is right. We lie with words, but also with silence.	• Definition of "lie" • Lying can also be done with silence	States another thesis ("Rich is right…")
For example, a man who knows he is HIV positive. He has unprotected sex with a woman but doesn't tell her he's HIV positive. As a result, she gets infected—and doesn't even know it. And then she can infect others. A chain reaction—a very deadly one.	Not telling HIV positive	Provides example of second thesis
I'm guilty, too. I knew my friend's boyfriend was also seeing someone else. But I kept quiet. I helped to keep her in the dark. Then, when she found him out—and found out I'd known about it—it was terrible. It destroyed their relationship, and our friendship.	Personal experience with Amy	Provides example of second thesis

This glossing reveals some very helpful information. You can see that the writer really has *two* introductions. The first two paragraphs each have what seems like a thesis statement: "This kind of lie can be even more devastating" and "Rich is right. We lie with words, but also with silence." The second thesis directly addresses the assignment, which is to agree or disagree with Rich's quote. But the first thesis is the idea the writer really wants to develop. Fortunately, these two ideas can be combined into one thesis. Here's how she revised her thesis:

We lie with words, but also with silence. And sometimes our silent lies can be even more devastating.

CHECKING FOR SUPPORT

Next, it's time to assess how well your draft supports your thesis. See Lesson 10 if you need a quick review of how to provide support. Types of evidence you can use to support your ideas include:

- specific examples
- facts
- reasons
- descriptions and anecdotes
- expert opinion and analysis
- quotations from the text

How Much Is Enough?

As usual, there is no hard and fast rule about how much support you need for an effective essay. Still, it's safe to say that one supporting idea is almost never enough. Two is better, but it may not be enough to be convincing. Three is often the magic number—it has "critical mass," and it *shows* readers why you think what you do. Four is even better; more than just critical mass, it's a good solid amount of evidence. The essay about "lying with silence" comes up a bit short in the amount of support it offers; there are two examples of silent lies. Three or four would be much better.

Support That's Directly Related to the Thesis

As important as the amount of support is its relevance to the thesis. What good are ten supporting paragraphs if they support a different idea? If you look closely at the two supporting examples in the "lying with silence" essay, you can see that neither example addresses how these silent lies are more devastating than a spoken lie. Now the writer must make a decision. Should she expand each paragraph to explain how keeping silent was worse than lying out loud? Or should she revise her thesis to eliminate the idea that silent lies are "more devastating" than regular lies?

Choosing the latter, she revised her thesis once more and crafted the following thesis statement:

We lie with words, but also with silence. And these lies can be equally devastating.

Now the writer has two solid supporting examples for her thesis. But she should probably add at least one more, preferably two, to strengthen her essay.

PRACTICE 1

So far there are only two supporting paragraphs for the "lying with silence" draft. Add an additional supporting paragraph to strengthen this essay.

_____

_____

_____

_____

_____

Strategies for Convincing

While this essay now has a clear, focused thesis supported by several examples, it still lacks persuasive power. Before you consider your check for support complete, consider whether or not you've applied the strategies for convincing that were discussed in Lesson 10. Ask yourself the following questions:

- Are your supporting paragraphs specific?
- Do you have any unsupported statements?
- Have you established credibility?
- Do you acknowledge counterarguments?
- Do you make concessions?
- Do you avoid absolutes?
- Do you say anything that might offend?

The "lying with silence" essay, for example, is not terribly specific in either of its examples. Each of these examples, in fact, should probably be two or three paragraphs not just one. More information would bring each example to life and show readers how people are affected by this kind of lie; more detail would help readers relate to the liars and their victims. And because this essay's support will come almost entirely in the form of specific examples, the more detailed those examples are, the more powerful the essay will be.

PRACTICE 2

On a separate sheet of paper or on your computer, revise one of the example paragraphs in the "lying with silence" essay to provide more information and specific details. Expand the example until you have two complete paragraphs.

IN SHORT

Revision deals with the content and style of the essay and should begin by addressing the big picture issues: thesis and support. Gloss your essay to see what ideas you develop in your draft and how well they support your thesis. Check that you have enough support and that you've applied the strategies for convincing.

Skill Building Until Next Time

Gloss an essay that you're working on or that you wrote for another occasion.

REVISING PARAGRAPHS

15

LESSON SUMMARY

This lesson shows you how to revise paragraphs for more effective organization and transitions. You'll also learn how to strengthen individual paragraphs.

Now that you've checked for a clear thesis and strong support, it's time to look carefully at your paragraphs. The first question to ask about paragraphs is also a question about the big picture:

1. Are your paragraphs in a logical and effective order?

Once you've addressed this question, then you can look at each paragraph individually with the following questions in mind:

2. Does each paragraph have only one controlling idea?

3. Are there effective transitions between ideas?

4. Do special paragraphs fulfill their functions?

CHECKING YOUR ORGANIZATION

You saw some of the benefits of glossing in Lesson 14. Now here's another: By showing which ideas you discuss where, glossing helps you assess your

essay's organization. You can see when you jump back and forth between ideas or when your ideas are out of order (for example, not chronological or in order of importance).

As mentioned earlier, most writers use a combination of organizational strategies throughout an essay. Still, they usually have one principle strategy organizing the essay as a whole. This main organizing strategy creates a logical relationship between your ideas and sets them up in a logical progression, making them much easier to follow. This also helps readers anticipate what's next in your essay. As a reminder, here are the seven organizing principles discussed in Lessons 6 and 7:

- chronology
- cause and effect
- spatial order
- analysis/classification
- order of importance
- comparison and contrast
- problem-solution

Once you've glossed your essay and revised for thesis and support, check for organization. (If you made substantial revision after checking for thesis and support, you need to do another glossing before checking the organization.) Consider the following questions:

1. **What organizing principle holds the essay together?** One overlying organizing principle should be clear. If you can't identify one, then you should look carefully at how you presented your ideas. If you haven't used an organizing strategy, chances are your essay will feel disjointed to readers. Think about which strategy makes the most sense for your subject and purpose.

2. **Is this the most effective organization for your subject and purpose?** Once you've identified your organizing principle, consider whether it's the best one for your essay. For example, if you've used the block technique for a comparison and contrast essay, you might consider whether the point-by-point method would work better instead.

3. **Do any paragraphs or sections disrupt this organizational pattern?** If you've set up an organizational structure and then break it, it'd better be for good reason. Otherwise, you should revise. For example, say you've decided to stick with your block comparison and contrast. In one section, though, you slip into the point-by-point mode and compare two items directly. Revise your essay so that it is consistent and all paragraphs use the block technique.

PRACTICE 1

Substantial revisions have been made to the essay about "lying with silence." First, gloss the revised essay. Then, answer the questions that follow. The first two paragraphs have been glossed to get you started.

Paragraph	Idea	Function
When was the last time you told a lie? If you're like most people, it was probably pretty recently. In fact, it was probably more recently than you think. The poet Adrienne Rich said that "Lying is done with words and also with silence." We don't have to talk to tell a lie. Our silences can be just as deceiving—and just as devastating.	Lying is also done with silence and can be devastating.	introduces the essay
You might be wondering how we can lie with silence. To lie means "to tell something that is untrue." But it also means "to be deceptive." There are many ways we deceive. Words are one way; silence is another.	definition of lie	explains how silence is also a lie
There's a difference between being silent because you don't want someone to know something and being silent because you want someone to think something that isn't true. The first is not a lie; it is not deceptive. The second, however, is a lie; the aim is to deceive. For example, imagine that I am in a job interview. If I don't tell you that I went to three different colleges, that's not a lie. But say I know you assume that I've graduated. If I don't tell you that I don't actually have a college degree, I am deliberately deceiving you with my silence. I am "telling" you a lie.		
These silent lies can have devastating consequences. For example, take a man who knows he is HIV positive. He has unprotected sex with a woman but doesn't tell her he's HIV positive. By not telling her he is infected, he lets her believe that he is not carrying the AIDS virus. As a result, she gets infected—and doesn't even know it.		
This man has committed a terrible crime with his silence. By remaining silent, he not only endangers the woman's life, he also endangers the life of anyone she may be intimate with in the future. In turn, they endanger everyone they're intimate with—and don't even know it.		

Paragraph	Idea	Function
I'm guilty of silent deceptions, too. For example, last year, I discovered that my friend Amy's boyfriend, Scott, was seeing someone else on the side. But I kept quiet about it because I didn't want to hurt Amy. A few weeks later, someone else told her about Scott's two-timing—and told her that I knew about it. Amy couldn't believe that I deceived her like that. She felt just as betrayed as if I'd lied to her face about it. Scott's deception ruined their relationship. My deception destroyed our friendship.		
Here's another example. Imagine you're at a diner. When the waitress hands you your check, you notice that she made a mistake, charging you $12.58 instead of $15.58. But you don't tell her. Instead, you pay $12.58 and pocket the $3.00 difference.		
Thus, as you can see, lies can be told with silence as well as with words. These lies can be just as devastating. That's why we should prosecute people who lie about their HIV status as murderers in the first degree.		

Questions

1. What is the main organizing principle of this essay?

   _____

2. Is this the best organizing strategy for this essay? Why or why not?

   _____

3. What would you suggest the writer do to improve the organization?

   _____

CHECKING INDIVIDUAL PARAGRAPHS

Now it's time to turn your attention to the individual paragraphs that make up your essay.

ONE CONTROLLING IDEA

Just as glossing can show you if you have more than one main idea in your essay, it can show you if you have more than one controlling idea in a paragraph. Remember, a paragraph is a series of sentences about *one idea*. If there's more than one main idea, you should probably have more than one paragraph.

One way to address this issue is to check for topic sentences. Go through each paragraph and underline the topic sentence. If you can't, then take a close look at that paragraph. Is there a controlling idea? If so, should it be stated in a topic sentence instead of just being implied? If there is no controlling idea, what purpose are those sentences serving? Would they make sense in other paragraphs throughout the essay? Or do they simply not belong?

In the "lying with silence" essay, each paragraph contains only one main idea except for the sixth paragraph. Here, she describes the lie and its consequences in one paragraph. It would probably be more effective to dedicate one paragraph to each issue, as in the previous example. The revised paragraphing for this example then looks like the following (the topic sentences are in boldface):

> ***I'm guilty of silent deceptions, too.*** *For example, last year, I discovered that my friend Amy's boyfriend, Scott, was seeing someone else on the side. But I kept quiet about it because I didn't want to hurt Amy. A few weeks later, someone else told her about Scott's two-timing—and told her that I knew about it.*

> *Amy couldn't believe that I deceived her like that. She felt just as betrayed as if I'd lied to her face about it. Scott's deception ruined their relationship.* ***My deception destroyed our friendship.***

Relevance

If you've identified more than one main idea, you should probably break that paragraph into two. But before you divide any paragraphs, it's a good idea to make sure that each main idea is clearly related to the thesis. If it's not, then it probably doesn't belong in your essay. (If you didn't eliminate unrelated paragraphs when you were revising the big picture, here's your chance to do so.) Remember, it's important to maintain focus in your essay—unrelated paragraphs not only get you off track but often confuse readers as well.

Development

Once you have identified the controlling idea of each paragraph, check to see that each idea is sufficiently developed. Remember, topic sentences, like thesis statements, make assertions about your subject. And those assertions need support. Look carefully at any paragraph that consists of only one or two sentences. Chances are they're seriously underdeveloped. Remember, the only time you should have a one-sentence paragraph is when you really want to emphasize that idea.

TRANSITIONS

Transitions are the words and phrases used to move from one idea to the next. Transitions help your words flow smoothly and show readers how your ideas relate to each other. In shorter essays, a short phrase or sentence is usually enough to transition from one paragraph to the next. Occasionally, however, especially in longer essays,

a whole paragraph may be required to get the job done. In all essays, transitions *within* paragraphs are as important as transitions *between* paragraphs, and you need to check for both as you revise.

Certain transitional words and phrases are particularly good for certain organizational strategies and functions. When you've organized something chronologically, for example, words like "then," "next," "before," and so on are the most helpful. Below is a list of many transitional words and phrases and what they're most often used for.

Organizing Principle	Transitional Words and Phrases		
order of importance	more importantly	above all	moreover
	in addition	first and foremost	furthermore
	first, second, third, etc.		
chronological	then	next	later
	before	after	during
	while	as	when
	afterwards	since	until
	first, second, third, etc.		
spatial	beside	next to	along
	around	above	below
	beyond	behind	in front of
	under	near	
cause and effect	therefore	because	as a result
	so	since	thus
	consequently	accordingly	hence
comparison	likewise	similarly	like
	in the same way	just as	
contrast	on the other hand	however	on the contrary
	unlike	but	yet
	rather	instead	whereas
	although		

Similarly, certain transitions work best for specific functions. For example, "for example" is a great transition to use when introducing a specific example. Here's another helpful list:

If You Want To	Use These Transitional Words and Phrases		
introduce an example	for example	for instance	that is
	in other words	in particular	specifically
	in fact	first (second) of all	
show addition	and	in addition	also
	again	moreover	furthermore
show emphasis	indeed	in fact	certainly
acknowledge another point of view	although	though	granted
	despite	even though	

In the "lying with silence" essay, notice how the writer uses transitions to move from one paragraph to another. For example, look at the sixth paragraph. The opening sentence, "I'm guilty of silent deceptions, too" connects the previous example (the man who didn't reveal that he was HIV positive) to the next example: the writer's own silent lie. Then, the beginning of the second sentence uses the transitional phrase "for example" to lead readers into the specific example. Further, the phrase "a few weeks later" provides a transition in the middle of the paragraph, connecting the writer's decision to keep silent with her friend's discovery of the deception.

To demonstrate how important transitions are, here's the fourth paragraph of the "lying with silence" essay first with its transitions removed, then reprinted with its transitions intact (and underlined):

Take a man who knows he is HIV positive. He has unprotected sex with a woman but doesn't tell her he's HIV positive. She gets infected—and doesn't even know it. He not only endangers her life, he endangers the life of anyone she may be intimate with in the future. They endanger everyone they're intimate with—and don't even know it.

These silent lies can have devastating consequences. For example, take a man who knows he is HIV positive. He has unprotected sex with a woman but doesn't tell her he's HIV positive. As a result, she gets infected—and doesn't even know it. By remaining silent, he not only endangers her life, he also endangers the life of anyone she may be intimate with in the future. In turn, they endanger everyone they're intimate with—and don't even know it.

SPECIAL PARAGRAPHS

There are two kinds of "special" paragraphs—paragraphs that have specific functions and require a unique approach. They are special enough to have gotten individual lessons in this book, and they're important enough to warrant special attention in the revising process. They are, of course, the paragraphs that introduce and conclude your essay.

Introductory Paragraphs

Remember, first impressions count, and count for a lot. Reread your essay's introduction. Then, answer the questions that follow:

- Does it provide the context needed to understand your thesis?
- Does it clearly state the main point of your essay?
- Does it set the tone for the essay?
- Does it grab your readers' interest?

Notice how the introduction to the "lying with silence" essay accomplishes each of these four tasks. It provides context by quoting Adrienne Rich's claim about silent deceptions. It clearly states the thesis in the last two sentences. It also sets the tone by using words like "deceives" and "devastating." And it grabs the reader's attention by opening up with a question that's bound to get readers thinking.

Concluding Paragraphs

Your conclusion is your last chance to make your point and make an impression on your reader. Take a careful look at your conclusion and ask yourself:

- Does it restate the thesis in a new way?
- Does it offer a new understanding?
- Does it provide a sense of closure?
- Does it arouse readers' emotions?

While the "lying with silence" essay does a good job with its introduction, its conclusion needs a lot of work. Notice how it simply repeats the thesis instead of restating it in a new way. It does offer a new understanding, but it goes too far, opening up a contentious new issue instead of providing a sense of closure.

PRACTICE 2

On a separate sheet of paper or your computer, revise the conclusion to the "lying with silence" essay.

IN SHORT

To revise on the paragraph level, first check for your overall organizing principle. How have you arranged your paragraphs? Is this the most effective organizing strategy for your essay? Then check individual paragraphs to make sure they have only one relevant and fully developed idea. Next, check for transitions both between and within paragraphs. Finally, check to see that your introduction and conclusion fulfill their special functions.

Skill Building Until Next Time

Look again at the essay that you glossed for the Skill Building Until Next Time segment in Lesson 14. Identify the organizing principle, the topic sentences, and the transitions used throughout the essay.

L·E·S·S·O·N

REVISING SENTENCES

16

LESSON SUMMARY

Now that you've revised the big picture and looked at your paragraphs, it's time to focus on your sentences. This lesson will show you how to revise sentences for clarity and style.

Though you may have a clear thesis and strong support, and though your paragraphs may be well organized with strong transitions between them, you're not done revising yet. For your *ideas* to come across clearly, your individual *sentences* need to be clear. This lesson will cover four strategies for writing clear sentences. You'll also learn some strategies for writing with style so your ideas will come across clearly and smoothly.

REVISING FOR CLARITY

Clarity is the quality of being clear—a very desirable characteristic for an essay. When you are ready to revise on the sentence level, follow these four rules of thumb for clear sentences:

1. Be concise.

2. Avoid jargon and pretentious language.

3. Use active rather than passive sentences.

4. Avoid ambiguity.

BE CONCISE

On the sentence level, in general, less is more. The fewer words you use to get your point across, the better. Unnecessary words frustrate readers—they waste time and often cloud meaning. To eliminate wordiness, eliminate clutter and unnecessary repetition in your sentences.

Eliminate Clutter

Avoid the following words, phrases, and constructions that add clutter to your writing.

1. **Because of the fact that** is an unnecessary and bulky phrase. "Because" is all you really need:

   Because of the fact that Willy Loman realizes he's been living a lie, he commits suicide in the play's final scene. (21 words)

   Because Willy Loman realizes he's been living a lie, he commits suicide in the play's final scene. (17 words)

2. *That, who,* and *which* **phrases** often clutter needlessly and can usually be rephrased more concisely. Try turning the *that, who,* or *which* phrase into an adjective:

   It was an experience *that was very rewarding.* (8 words)
   It was a *very rewarding* experience. (6 words)

3. **There is, it is.** The *there is* and *it is* constructions avoid directly approaching the subject and use unnecessary words in the process. Instead, use a clear agent of action:

   It was with much regret that I had to postpone my education. (12 words)
   I greatly regretted having to postpone my education. (8 words)
   Regrettably, I had to postpone my education. (7 words)

   There is no reason for people to protest this policy. (10 words)
   People have no reason to protest this policy. (8 words)

4. **That** is a word that often clutters sentences unnecessarily. Sentences will often read more smoothly without it:

   I wish *that* I had taken the opportunity *that* I was given more seriously. (14 words)
   I wish I had taken the opportunity I was given more seriously. (12 words)
   I wish I had taken the opportunity more seriously. (9 words)

5. **I am of the opinion that, I believe, I feel,** and other similar phrases are unnecessary unless you are distinguishing between what *you* think and what someone else thinks. Remember, essays are about what you think, so readers expect that you say what you believe.

> *I am of the opinion that* the flat tax is a good idea. (13 words)
> *I feel that* the flat tax is a good idea. (10 words)
> *I believe* the flat tax is a good idea. (9 words)
> The flat tax is a good idea. (7 words)

Avoid Unnecessary Repetition

When writers are not sure they've been clear, or when they are simply not being attentive to the need for concise writing, they often repeat themselves unnecessarily by saying the same thing in two different ways. This is what happened in the following example:

> The willow beetle is red in color and large in size. (11 words)

Red *is* a color, so there's no need to say "in color." Likewise, large *is* a size—so "in size" is a waste of words. Here's the sentence revised:

> The willow beetle is red and large. (7 words)

Here's another example of unnecessary repetition:

> The Bill of Rights guarantees certain freedoms and liberties to all citizens, rights that cannot be taken away. (18 words)

If it's a guarantee, then those rights cannot be taken away—so the whole second half of the sentence repeats unnecessarily. Similarly, "freedom" and "liberties" are essentially the same thing, so only one of those words is necessary. Here's the sentence revised:

> The Bill of Rights guarantees certain freedoms to all citizens. (10 words)

AVOID JARGON AND PRETENTIOUS LANGUAGE

Back in Lesson 1, you learned that you should never assume your reader is as familiar with your subject matter as you are. That's why it's important to avoid jargon. Jargon is technical or specialized language used by a limited audience. For example, you may know what a T-cell count is, but unless your readers have had some experience with physiology, AIDS, or other infectious diseases, chances are *they* don't know.

The same caution goes for abbreviations and acronyms. You may know what RAM is, but you can't assume your readers do. Always write out what the abbreviation or acronym stands for the first time you use it. Then, going forward, you can use the abbreviation or acronym. Here's an example:

When buying a home computer, you need to consider how much random access memory (RAM) you need. The amount of RAM you should have depends upon what kind of programs your machine will be running.

If you find jargon in your draft, you have two choices: either replace the words with a general word or phrase that readers will know, or keep the technical term, but define it. Here's an example:

Bobby's T-cell count (the number of infection-fighting white blood cells) fell dangerously low. With his weakened immune system, it was just a matter of time before he succumbed to an infection.

Pretentious language is another matter. Pretentious means showy or pompous. Some people are impressed with big words, as if the more syllables you use in your sentences, the more intelligent you must be. Sometimes a big, multisyllabic word is the one that most clearly expresses the idea you want to convey, and that's fine. But what good are five-syllable words if you don't use them properly, or if they hamper understanding instead of aiding it? It's clear writing, not big words, that really impresses readers. In any case, there's no need for a sentence like the following:

Utilizing my cognitive facilities, I ruminated upon the matter.

Instead of sounding impressive, this sentence sounds a bit foolish. A simple, more direct sentence like the following does the trick much more effectively:

I thought about it.

USE THE ACTIVE VOICE

Using the active voice means making sure a sentence has a clear agent of action and a direct approach. For example, compare the following sentences:

Passive: The patient was given the wrong prescription.

Active: Someone gave the patient the wrong prescription.

Notice how the active sentence gives readers an agent of action—a person, place, or thing that performs the action in the sentence. In the passive sentence, you don't know who or what gave the patient the wrong prescription; you just know that somehow it happened. The active sentence may not name the "someone," but it is a much more direct sentence. The active voice also makes a sentence sound more authoritative and powerful—*someone* is doing *something*. In a passive sentence, someone or something has something done *to* it.

There are times when using the passive voice makes more sense than trying to write an active sentence—like when you don't know the agent of action or when you want to emphasize the action, not the agent. It's also useful when you desire anonymity or objectivity. Here are two examples:

The location was deemed suitable by the commission. (Here, the passive voice emphasizes the action of the commission rather than the commission itself.)

He was fired. (The passive voice provides anonymity by not giving an agent of action. Thus, no one has to take the blame for firing him.)

AVOID AMBIGUITY

Ambiguous means having two or more possible meanings, so of course ambiguous words and phrases interfere with clarity. Take a look at this sentence, for example:

The photographer shot the model.

This sentence can be read in two ways: that the photographer took ("shot") pictures of the model with his camera, or that he shot the model with a gun. You can eliminate this ambiguity by revising the sentence as follows:

The photographer *took pictures* of the model.

"Took pictures" isn't as powerful a phrase as the verb "shot," but at least there's no ambiguity.

Another type of ambiguity happens when a phrase is in the wrong place in a sentence. For example, look at the following sentence:

The woman ate the sandwich with the blue hat.

Here, the *word order*, not an ambiguous word, causes the confusion. Did the woman eat her sandwich with her hat? Or was the woman wearing a blue hat as she ate the sandwich? Because the phrase "with a blue hat" is in the wrong place, the sentence becomes unclear. The sentence should be revised to read:

The woman with a blue hat ate the sandwich.

Unclear Pronoun References

Ambiguity also results from unclear pronoun references. Pronouns are the words used to replace nouns (I, you, he, she, it, we, they,). Here's an example of an unclear pronoun reference:

In *Heart of Darkness,* Conrad has Kurtz tell Marlow his revelation right before he dies on the steamboat.

There are three different people each pronoun could be referring to: Conrad, Kurtz, and Marlow. Clearly, this sentence needs to be revised:

In Conrad's *Heart of Darkness,* Kurtz tells Marlow his revelation right before Kurtz dies on the steamboat.

Here's another kind of unclear pronoun reference:

It's been years since *they* tore down that old building.

This is an example of a common pronoun error: using a vague "they" when there are specific people behind the action. You may not know exactly who those people are, but you know enough to say something like the following:

It's been years since *a demolition crew* tore down that building.

There are always people behind their actions, and your sentences should say so.

PRACTICE 1

Revise the paragraph below for clarity. Eliminate wordiness, jargon, pretentious language, passive sentences, and ambiguity.

I believe that the biggest and greatest challenge my generation will face will be ethical dilemmas created by scientific discoveries and advances. There is so much that has been discovered in this century, especially in the time period of the last few decades. Humankind is able to avail itself of a plethora of opportunities it heretofore was unable to take advantage of. But some very difficult ethical questions have been raised by these opportunities. They have given us new power over nature, but this power can easily be abused and misused.

REVISING YOUR STYLE

Style is the manner in which something is done. For example, two people can sing the same song, but they will do it in different ways—according to their own style. In writing, style is created by several different elements. You'll learn about two of them in this lesson: word choice and sentence structure.

WORD CHOICE

An essay has more impact when it's filled with exact words and phrases. This means substituting a strong, specific word or phrase for a weak or modified word or phrase. (A modifier is a word that describes, like *red* balloon or *very juicy* apple.) A lot of wordiness can be trimmed by using exact words and phrases, too. Notice how attention to word choice cuts back on wordiness and creates much more powerful sentences in the example below:

He *walked quickly* into the room.

He *rushed* into the room.
He *raced* into the room.
He *dashed* into the room.
He *burst* into the room.

Each of these verbs has much more impact than the phrase "walked quickly." These exact verbs create a vivid picture; they tell readers exactly how he came into the room.

Exact nouns will improve your sentences, too. Here's an example:

The *dog* escaped down *the street*.
The *pit bull* escaped down *Elm Street*.

Again, the specific nouns help readers *see* what the writer is describing—they bring the sentence to life. Adjectives, too, should be precise. Instead of writing:

I am *very frightened*.

Try an exact adjective:

I am *petrified*.

Petrified means "very frightened"—and it's a much more powerful word.

SENTENCE STRUCTURE

Sometimes writers repeat a specific sentence pattern to create rhythm in their writing. This is called **parallelism**. Here's a famous example:

I came, I saw, I conquered.

Notice the basic sentence pattern: the subject ("I") + past-tense verb. This pattern is repeated three times, and the result is a certain controlled rhythm to the sentences. Here's another example:

Scott's deception ruined their relationship. My deception destroyed our friendship.

As you can see, parallelism consciously repeats a sentence pattern to create a positive effect. However, that's not always the case, as you can see from the following example:

The plasma membrane is the outermost part of the cell. It isolates the cytoplasm. It regulates what comes in and out of the cytoplasm. It also allows interaction with other cells. The cytoplasm is the second layer of the cell. It contains water, salt, enzymes and proteins. It also contains organelles like mitochondria.

Here, there's a certain rhythm to the sentences, but instead of creating energy, it creates monotony. Because there's no variety in the sentence structure, the paragraph's rhythm is more like a drone than a conversation. Here's the same paragraph revised to create sentence variety:

The plasma membrane, the outermost part of the cell, isolates the cytoplasm. It regulates what comes in and out of the cell and allows interaction with other cells. The second layer, the cytoplasm, contains water, salt, enzymes, and proteins as well as organelles like mitochondria.

This revised version combines sentences and uses introductory phrases and appositives (descriptive words and phrases set off by commas) to vary the sentence structure. The result is a much more engaging paragraph.

PRACTICE 2

Revise the following paragraph for style. Replace general words with more exact ones and combine or otherwise alter sentences to create sentence variety. (Note: You may have to revise for clarity, too, to address some of the problems in this paragraph.)

> My generation will have many problems. One is the feeling of being overwhelmed by technology. Another is that the generation gap is growing. Another is that there are more people than ever before. There isn't enough room for everybody. There are also limited resources.

IN SHORT

Wordiness and ambiguity often prevent ideas from coming across clearly. Revise your sentences to eliminate clutter words and phrases and any unnecessary repetition. Revise sentences that use jargon or pretentious language and turn passive sentences into active ones. Clarify ambiguous words and unclear pronoun references. Finally, improve your style by using exact words and phrases and adding variety to your sentence structure.

Skill Building Until Next Time

Try writing some really bad sentences. Use unnecessary words and repetition, jargon, pretentious language, unclear pronoun references, and ambiguous words. Steer clear of exact words and phrases and try for monotonous sentence structure. By trying to write badly, you'll get a better sense of what to avoid in your writing.

L·E·S·S·O·N

EDITING

17

LESSON SUMMARY

Before you submit your essay, there's one more important step: editing. This lesson explains the editing process and provides several strategies for effective editing.

You've planned, drafted, and revised your essay. You're satisfied that it says what you want it to say, how you want to say it. At last, you've come to the final step in the writing process: editing.

As explained in Lesson 14, **editing** is the process of cleaning up the **grammar**, **mechanics**, and **formatting** of your essay. It should be the *last* step in your writing process because you want to be sure you're working with sentences and paragraphs that aren't going to be changed any more. Imagine, for example, that you are cooking in the kitchen. You can do a limited amount of cleanup as you go along, but if you clean up everything, you'll end up washing and putting away certain items two, maybe even three times, because you're not done using them yet. The same goes for editing. Wait until you've finalized revising so that you don't have to edit again if you change your essay.

CHECKING FOR GRAMMAR

Grammar refers to the rules that govern sentences. This is not a grammar book, and there isn't room here to review all of the rules you've learned over the years in school. But because clean, clear writing is so important, this lesson covers three of the more common grammatical errors committed in essays:

- fragments
- run-on sentences
- tense shifts

FRAGMENTS

A complete sentence has a **subject** (who or what performs the action) and a **verb** (a state of being or an action). It also expresses a complete thought. If you don't complete a thought, or if you are missing a subject or verb (or both), then you have an incomplete sentence (also called a sentence fragment). To correct a fragment, add the missing subject or verb or otherwise change the sentence to complete the thought.

Incomplete: Which is true. [No subject. *Which* is not a subject.]
Complete: *That* is true.

Incomplete: For example, tree frogs and salamanders. [No verb]
Complete: Two examples *are* tree frogs and salamanders.

Incomplete: Even though Hiroshima was not a military target. [Subject and verb, but not a complete thought.]
Complete: The bomb was dropped even though Hiroshima was not a military target.

RUN-ON SENTENCES

A run-on sentence occurs when two or more sentences run together without the proper punctuation between them. Usually, this means there's either no punctuation or just a comma separating the two thoughts. But commas alone are not strong enough to place between two complete ideas.

There are five ways to correct run-on sentences:

1. with a period

2. with a comma and a conjunction: *and, or, nor, for, so, but, yet*

3. with a semi-colon

4. with a dash

5. with a dependent clause

Here's a run-on sentence corrected with each of the techniques listed above:

We have to recycle, our natural resources are limited.

1. We have to recycle. Our natural resources are limited.

2. We have to recycle, **for** our natural resources are limited.

3. We have to recycle; our natural resources are limited.

4. We have to recycle—our natural resources are limited.

5. We have to recycle **because** our natural resources are limited.

TENSE SHIFTS

A very common error, especially in narrative essays, is **shifting verb tenses**. That is, you start off telling a story in the present tense and then shift to the past tense (or vice versa). This kind of error is particularly common when students write about literature. Here's an example:

In *The Things They Carried,* Tim O'Brien tells the story of a soldier's experience with the Vietnam War. When the narrator (also named O'Brien) gets drafted, he thinks about crossing the border to Canada. He even took a boat across the lake, stopping just a few yards from the Canadian shoreline. He was ready to jump in and swim to Canada, but then he changes his mind. He decided he was too afraid of being called a coward, so he goes off to war.

Notice how this paragraph jumps back and forth between the present and past tense. The convention is to write about events that take place in a story or poem in the present tense. Thus, you can correct this paragraph as follows:

In *The Things They Carried,* Tim O'Brien tells the story of a soldier's experience with the Vietnam War. When the narrator (also named O'Brien) gets drafted, he thinks about crossing the border to Canada. He even takes a boat across the lake, stopping just a few yards from the Canadian shoreline. He is ready to jump in and swim to Canada, but then he changes his mind. He decides he is too afraid of being called a coward, so he goes to war.

PRACTICE 1

Edit the following paragraph for grammatical mistakes. Feel free to improve the clarity and style of the sentences as well.

Comic relief is important in tragedies, readers need a little relief from all of the sadness in the story. For example, Hamlet. Ophelia had just died. He next scene is with the grave digger. Who is a very funny character. He dug up a skull and makes a long speech about who the skull might have belonged to. Even though it is about death. The scene is funny, it lets readers forget about the tragedy for a moment and laugh.

CHECKING FOR MECHANICS

Mechanics refers to the standard practices for the presentation of words and sentences, including capitalization, punctuation, and spelling. This isn't a book about mechanics, either, but you may want to review a few of the basics. You will find a listing in the appendix of books on grammar and mechanics that give more detail.

CAPITALIZATION

The general rule for capitalization is this: If you are referring to a **specific** person, place, or thing, the word should be capitalized. If you are referring to a **general** person, place, or thing, the word should not be capitalized.

Incorrect: I've lived on a quiet, tree-lined Street all my life.

Correct: I've lived on quiet, tree-lined Elm Street all my life.

Correct: I've lived on a quiet, tree-lined street all my life.

Incorrect: My favorite subject has always been Math.

Correct: My favorite subject has always been math.

Note: Names of countries, languages, and nationalities should always be capitalized. Thus, if the sentence above read "My favorite subject has always been English," this sentence would be correct.

PUNCTUATION

Punctuation marks are the symbols used to separate ideas and make the meaning of sentences clear. Poor punctuation can lead to a great deal of confusion for your readers and can send a message other than what you intended. For example, take a look at the two versions of the following sentence:

Don't call me, stupid!

Don't call me stupid!

See what a difference punctuation can make? In the first sentence, the speaker is calling the listener "stupid." In the second sentence, the speaker is angry because the listener has called *him* "stupid."

There are many rules for punctuation, of course, and there isn't room to go into all of them here. However, the table below offers a few helpful guidelines for when to use which punctuation mark:

If Your Purpose Is To:	Use This Punctuation:	Example:
end a sentence	**period** [.]	Use a period to end a sentence.
connect complete sentences	**semicolon** [;] or a **comma** [,] *and* a **conjunction** [and, or, nor, for, so, but, yet]	A semi-colon can connect two sentences; it is an excellent way to show that two ideas are related.
connect items in a list	**comma** [,] but if one or more items in that list already has a comma, use a **semicolon** [;]	The table was overturned, the mattress was torn apart, and the dresser drawers were strewn all over the floor. The castaways included a professor, who was the group's leader; an actress; and a housewife.
introduce a quotation or explanation	**colon** [:] or **comma** [,]	Colons have three functions: introducing long lists, introducing quotations, and introducing explanations. He said, "This simply won't do."
indicate a quotation	**quotation marks** [" "]	"To be or not to be?" is one of the most famous lines from *Hamlet*.
indicate a question	**question mark** [?]	Why are so many engineering students obsessed with *Star Trek*?
connect two words that work together	**hyphen** [-]	brother-in-law, well-known author
separate a word or phrase for emphasis	**dash** [—]	I never lie—never.
separate a word or phrase that is relevant but not essential information	**parenthesis** [( )]	There is an exception to every rule (including this one).
show possession or contraction	**Apostrophe** [']	That's Jane's car.

SPELLING

Presentation counts, and sometimes it counts for a lot. Always check your essay for spelling and typographical errors. If you use a computer, run the spell check, or have someone else look over your document for spelling.

Even if you use spell check, make sure you read the text over, looking specifically for spelling errors and typos. Even the best spell check programs don't catch everything. For example, you may have typed "even" instead of "seven," but since "even" is a word, the spell checker won't catch that error for you.

Some writers find it easier to catch typos by "reading" backwards through the essay. Try this method if you think it might help.

PRACTICE 2

Edit the following paragraph for mechanical errors.

Did you no that before Galileo, most people beleived that the earth, was the center of the Universe. Galileo discovered many things including the telescope the Law of falling bodies and the Moons around jupiter. But Galileos most important discovery was definately the true structure of the solar system. He prooved that the planets revolve around the Sun; insted of everything revolving around the earth.

CHECKING FOR FORMAT

Finally, before you hand in your essay, check for proper formatting. What are the presentation requirements? Do you need to have a cover page? If so, what information should you include on that cover page? Do you have specific attachments that you need to include, like a works cited page or a bibliography? Make sure you know what's expected of you regarding presentation and format and follow those guidelines carefully.

Some assignments may not include information about format. In that case, follow these general formatting guidelines:

- Include page numbers (in the bottom center or bottom right hand corner of each page).
- Set 1 to $1\frac{1}{2}$ inch margins on all sides—no more, no less.
- Use a 10- or 12-point standard font, such as Times New Roman or Arial. Never use a font that's difficult to read, like Peignot or Compacta. They're fancy, but they're not reader friendly.
- Avoid having one line of a paragraph standing alone at the top or bottom of a page.
- Make sure you have a clean, clear printout to submit—no stray ink or pen marks, no food stains, no faded toner.
- Staple or otherwise fasten all the pages together so no sheets get lost.

IN SHORT

Editing is the final step in the writing process. Be on the lookout for fragments, run-ons, tense shifts, and other grammatical mistakes. Look carefully for errors in mechanics, including capitalization, spelling, and especially punctuation. Finally, be sure that you've followed all formatting and presentation guidelines.

Skill Building Until Next Time

Get a good grammar handbook and review the rules of grammar and mechanics. Pay particular attention to the sections that address your weak spots. If you tend to write sentence fragments, for example, spend extra time working through the exercises on complete sentences.

S·E·C·T·I·O·N 4

TAKING AN ESSAY EXAM

This fourth and final section deals with a specific essay writing situation: the notorious essay exam. Though you can still use most of the writing strategies you've learned so far, because your time is limited, this kind of essay requires a unique approach. The lessons in this section will give you specific strategies for tackling essay exams, from the crucial planning stage through the editing process.

L·E·S·S·O·N

PLANNING YOUR ESSAY

18

LESSON SUMMARY

As usual, there's a significant amount of work to do before you actually begin to draft your essay for an essay exam. This lesson explains how to prepare for an essay exam and how to plan your essay.

E ven students who are normally comfortable writing essays can have panic attacks when it comes to a timed essay exam. It's easy to understand why. In most cases, even if you have a general idea of the kind of essay assignment you may be given, you still don't know exactly what you'll have to write about, or how you'll have to address that topic. And "have to" is a key phrase. While you'll have some freedom with the specifics, you *must* write about a certain subject in a certain way if you want to earn credit for your essay. Worse, you only have a limited amount of time in which to write that essay.

WHY AN ESSAY EXAM?

Why put you through this ordeal, anyway? After all, when in the real world do you have to write something under so much time pressure? Actually, many jobs entail more writing than most people realize, and much of that writing often has to be done quickly. But that's only part of the point. More

importantly, by restricting the time and place in which you write, essay exams get a measure of the "true" you. That is, readers can be sure that the writing is entirely your own. In an essay exam, you can't get feedback from teachers, parents, friends—and you certainly can't download your essay from the Internet. In other words, essay exams reveal something about how you write in isolation.

Of course, real writing doesn't take place in a vacuum, and as you've learned throughout this book, the more feedback you can get along the way, the better. But an essay test measures how well you can organize and convey your ideas on your own. And if you can write effectively without feedback, this shows two things:

(1) you can make sense of your own thoughts

(2) you understand the needs of your audience

Of course, many essay exams also test your knowledge of a specific subject. Why give an essay exam instead of a multiple choice or fill-in-the-blank test? An essay allows you to *explain* what you know, to show your understanding of facts, processes, and relationships in a way that no other kind of test can come close to.

PREPARING FOR AN ESSAY EXAM

This section describes several steps to take before an essay exam.

DO YOUR HOMEWORK

Even if you only have 20 minutes to write, you should still start planning your essay long before the date of the exam. Find out as much as you can about what the exam will be like. You can significantly reduce your pre-test jitters by minimizing your "fear of the unknown" and learning what will be expected of you on the exam. For the SAT II, for example, you know you'll have 20 minutes to write a short essay on a broad topic. You know that there are two or three types of questions you may be asked. You also know that you can use your personal experience to respond to the question.

For subject matter tests, be sure to thoroughly review the material that you will be tested on. For the English AP exam, for example, you should know several works of literature well enough that you will feel comfortable discussing them—whatever the focus of the question may be.

RELAX

The more tense you are, the more likely you are to suffer from writer's block or to simply write badly. Try your best to relax. When you feel nervous, breathe deeply. Try five to ten deep breaths. It's time well spent. You not only help re-establish your body's equilibrium; you also give yourself a chance to clear your mind and refocus. And you may even come up with a great idea for your essay in the process.

THINK POSITIVELY

Reassure yourself with positive thoughts; get negative thoughts and criticisms out of your head. Remind yourself that you know what to expect and that you can handle the assignment.

SET A SCHEDULE

As soon as you know how much time you will have to write, set a schedule so that you can effectively manage your time. You should spend approximately $\frac{1}{4}$ of the time planning, $\frac{1}{2}$ of the time writing, and $\frac{1}{4}$ of the time revising and editing. If you can stick closely to your schedule, you won't end up running out of time before you've even come to your conclusion.

If you are given 20 minutes to write, then you should spend 5 minutes planning, 10 minutes writing, and 5 minutes revising and editing your essay. If the exam is an hour, plan for 10 to 15 minutes, write for 30 to 35 minutes, and revise and edit for the last 10 to 15 minutes.

Time Management

Set a schedule that allows time for each step in the writing process:

- Spend the first $\frac{1}{4}$ of your time planning your essay.
- Spend $\frac{1}{2}$ of your time drafting your essay.
- Spend the last $\frac{1}{4}$ of your time revising your essay.

TAKING AN ESSAY EXAM

Once you receive the exam, it's time to move—and move fast. This section gives you five strategies for how to effectively plan your essay.

STEP 1: BREAK DOWN THE ASSIGNMENT

As soon as you get the test, read the essay assignment and instructions carefully. Be sure you understand the assignment completely. What subjects must you address? How must you address it? Remember, in most cases, you will not receive credit—however wonderful your essay—if you do not fulfill the assignment. Also, be sure to read all guidelines regarding formatting and any other procedures carefully. You might, for example, be required to submit an outline. You could also be asked to write on only one side of the page or only on every other line. Your readers probably have good reason for asking you to follow certain procedures, and they will be looking to see whether or not you followed directions.

If you are unclear about *any* aspect of the assignment, ask for clarification. Don't assume that "close enough" is "good enough"—chances are it may not be.

STEP 2: CHOOSE YOUR TOPIC QUICKLY

While it's important to pick the right topic, you don't have time to dally. Make your decision quickly. If you have a list of topics to choose from, pick the one that you know the most about. If you have a general topic (for example, an accomplishment you are proud of or an example of "mind over matter"), do a *quick* brainstorm to generate ideas. Try a one-minute freewrite, a short list, or a quick map. As soon as you get an idea that you're interested in and that meets the assignment, go with it.

STEP 3: FORMULATE A TENTATIVE THESIS

As soon as you choose a topic, draft a thesis statement. Make sure it's assertive and clear. Double check that it meets the requirements of the assignment.

STEP 4: CREATE A DETAILED OUTLINE

This step is essential. Unless you have more than an hour to write one essay, you probably don't have time to do a rough draft and then revise it. A much more effective strategy is to write a very detailed outline that serves as your "rough draft." List all of the ideas you plan to use to support your thesis. Get detailed; the more detailed, the better. If you do it right, you'll end up with a point in your outline for just about every sentence in your essay.

STEP 5: REVISE YOUR OUTLINE

Before you begin to write, check your outline for the big picture issues you'd normally address during the revising process:

1. Does your essay fulfill the assignment?

2. Do you have one clear main idea?

3. Have you effectively supported that idea? Is your support convincing?

4. Are your ideas organized in an effective and logical way?

Checking your outline *before* you draft will make your writing time much more productive and can save you a lot of revising work later.

For example, imagine you're taking the SAT II. You know you have about five minutes to plan before you need to begin writing. Here's your assignment:

"Problems are opportunities in disguise." Write an essay in which you agree or disagree with this statement. Use an example from your personal experience, current events, history, literature, or another discipline to support your answer. Use the following space to write your answer.

First, you should quickly break down the assignment:

Subject	Directions
Whether "problems are opportunities in disguise."	Agree or disagree; use an example to support.

Second, you might do a one-minute freewrite like the following:

Problems are opportunities . . . what is a problem? A situation you don't like, you want it to be different. And you have to figure out a way to change it. To solve problems sometimes you have to learn new things. Like last week, our sink. I had to learn how to fix it. Or when my car broke down. I had to learn how to drive a stick shift.

Third, you should formulate a thesis statement like the following:

We should embrace problems, because they are opportunities to learn about ourselves, others, and the world around us.

Fourth, you need to develop a detailed outline:

Introduction: *How do you feel about problems?*

Thesis: *We should embrace them. They're opportunities to learn.*

Example: *My family's problem: the leak in the sink*

- *Needed immediate attention*
  - *Dishes to wash, water all over the floor*
- *Landlord was out of town*
- *Couldn't afford a plumber ourselves*
- *Went to library*
  - *Found some do-it-yourself books*
  - *Learned what the problem was*
- *Fixed it!*
  - *Felt great about it*

Conclusion: *Problems make life interesting. They help us grow.*

Finally, you should check the outline for big picture issues. You might consider, for example, that there's no place in this outline where you address counterarguments. You might add a bullet that acknowledges that not all problems *seem* like opportunities, and it may be a long time before you realize what you were able to get out of the situation. Otherwise, you have good chronological order and your outline clearly fulfills the assignment. (You'll see the results of this outline in Lesson 20.)

PRACTICE

Set a timer for five minutes. Draft a thesis statement and create an outline for the following sample SAT II essay assignment:

> *Some people say there are no more heroes, but I see plenty of heroic people all around me. One person I consider a hero is _____.*
>
> *Fill in the blank in the sentence above. Write an essay in which you explain your answer.*

In Short

To help you do your best on an essay exam, start by learning as much as you can about the kind of assignment you'll be given and prepare appropriately. If you know what to expect and you've done your homework, you can relax and think positively during the exam. During the test, manage your time by setting a schedule. Be sure you understand the assignment clearly and choose your topic quickly. Draft a thesis and then create a very detailed outline to serve as your rough draft.

Skill Building Until Next Time

Because essay exams are timed, they challenge your ability to think on your feet. Play a game like Scategories, Taboo, or other game that uses a timer. These games force you to think and react quickly.

L · E · S · S · O · N

DRAFTING, REVISING, AND EDITING

LESSON SUMMARY

This lesson explains how to spend the other three-quarters of your essay exam time: drafting and revising your essay.

ou've chosen a topic, drafted a thesis statement, and created a detailed outline. Now it's time to write.

DRAFTING THE ESSAY

Probably the most important thing to remember during an essay exam is that unless you have a lot of time to write, you cannot treat this step as a rough draft. Since your revising time will be severely limited, your writing has to be considerably more refined than it might be in a typical rough draft. Below are a few general guidelines to help you through this kind of drafting process.

GENERAL GUIDELINES
Stick to Your Outline

Unless you see a major flaw in your outline, or unless you think of a better supporting idea or example, follow your outline as closely as possible as you write. Stay open to better ideas, but use your outline to keep yourself moving.

Be Quick but Thorough

Remember, you don't have the time to write a rough draft, where you can leave sections sketchy or blank and fill them in later. Complete your essay section by section as best as you can.

Keep Moving

While you may need to pause momentarily to gather your thoughts or consider the best way to express an idea, it's important to keep moving. You shouldn't have to stop to think of examples or evidence because you did that when you created your outline. Instead, focus on writing clear and correct sentences. If you have trouble expressing a thought, don't get stuck on it. Remember, you don't have time to waste. Instead, approximate—write something close to what you want to say. If you have time when you've finished writing, you can go back to that sentence and revise it. If not, at least you'll have something close on paper.

Avoid "Filler" Sentences

Don't waste time (yours or your reader's) by writing empty sentences, like "This is a very interesting question" or "Different people have different opinions on this issue." Make each sentence count; say something meaningful about your topic.

Write Neatly

An essay with great content won't do you much good if your readers can't decipher your handwriting. And, for better or worse, some exam readers may be unconsciously influenced by your penmanship. If two essays are of equal quality, and one is written neatly, the other in a rushed, sloppy hand, chances are the neatly written essay will receive a slightly higher score than the sloppy one. The neat handwriting is more reader friendly, and it suggests that the writer has more control over the writing process. In contrast, sloppy handwriting suggests that the writer had some trouble getting his or her ideas together and had to rush through the essay. This inference may be far from the truth, but it's how your essay may be perceived. So if you're a notoriously sloppy scribe, try to neaten up—but only so much that it doesn't slow you down.

SPECIAL PARAGRAPHS

Your introductory and concluding paragraphs, as usual, need some special attention. Below are some strategies to employ.

Introduction

- Don't simply repeat the question or assignment. If you really want to, you can rephrase it, but you're better off simply stating your answer to the question (your thesis) in a clear, assertive sentence.
- If you can't think of a catchy way to begin, skip the introduction. Leave space and come back to it later. Move right on to the body of the essay so you can get some momentum going (and so you don't waste any more time). In the worst case, if you run out of time, you can always go back and simply fill in your thesis statement.
- Don't forget to provide context. Of course your readers will know the assignment that you've been given, but remember, unless the assignment specifies otherwise, you should write for a general audience.

Conclusion

- Avoid simply repeating the thesis; instead, restate it in other words.
- Don't forget to offer a new understanding (your "gift" to the reader).
- Try to frame your essay. Since you're short on time, and since framing brings such a nice sense of closure, don't spend time thinking about how to close—go back to your introduction for inspiration.

REVISING AND EDITING THE ESSAY

If you put together a thorough outline and checked it for big picture issues in the planning stage—and if you stuck to your outline—you should now be able to focus on revising your paragraphs and sentences. Here are some questions to ask yourself as you revise:

INDIVIDUAL PARAGRAPHS

1. Does each paragraph have one controlling idea?

2. Is that idea clearly related to the thesis?

3. Is that idea fully developed?

4. Are there effective transitions between ideas?

5. Do special paragraphs fulfill their functions?

SENTENCES

1. Are your sentences concise?

2. Do you avoid jargon and pretentious language?

3. Are your sentences active rather than passive?

4. Do any sentences contain ambiguity?

5. Do you use exact words and phrases?

6. Do you have variety in your sentence structure?

GRAMMAR, MECHANICS, AND FORMAT

1. Are all of your sentences complete?

2. Do you have any run-on sentences?

3. Do you shift tenses?

4. Are the proper words capitalized? Do you have any unnecessary capitalization?

5. Do you use the proper punctuation between ideas?

6. Have you spelled words correctly?

7. Have you followed the formatting guidelines for your essay?*

*Again, make sure you understand the formatting requirements *before* you begin to write. If you are supposed to write only on one side of the page, for example, but don't realize this until *after* you've already written on both sides, it's too late to correct your mistake.

PRACTICE

Make sure you can have peace and quiet for at least 20 minutes before you begin this exercise. Resist the urge to read ahead and start thinking about the assignment before you're actually ready to do it. When you're ready, set a timer for 20 minutes. Then, take the essay exam on the next page.

> **STOP! Don't read the topic until you are ready to write for 20 minutes.**

"Ignorance is bliss." Write an essay in which you agree or disagree with this statement. Use an example from your personal experience, current events, history, literature, or another discipline to support your answer. Use the following space to write your answer. Do not write on any other topic; do not use any additional paper; do not skip lines.

_____

_____

_____

_____

_____

_____

_____

_____

_____

_____

_____

_____

_____

_____

_____

_____

_____

_____

_____

_____

_____

_____

_____

_____

_____

IN SHORT

On an essay exam, you need a draft that is already well developed and somewhat polished. Follow your detailed outline and write carefully but quickly. Make sure your thoughts are complete and your handwriting neat. If you can't think of how to begin, leave some space for your introduction and start writing the body of your essay. If you revised your outline for big picture issues, then you can focus your revision process on making sure you have clear, strong paragraphs and sentences.

Skill Building Until Next Time

Like all skills, your ability to write well under time pressure will only improve with practice. Choose one of the essay topics from the introduction to this book (or from any other chapter, for that matter), set a timer for 30 or 40 minutes, and write another essay (or two, or three . . . the more, the better).

L·E·S·S·O·N 20

SAMPLE ESSAY EXAM QUESTIONS AND ANSWERS

LESSON SUMMARY

This final lesson presents two sample essay exam assignments and several sample responses. The answers are analyzed to give you a clearer sense of what makes a good essay (and what doesn't).

Whenever you're asked to do something, it's often helpful to see how others have performed a similar task. That's why this final lesson is devoted to showing you sample essay exam assignments and responses. There are two sample exams, and you'll see a total of five sample answers to cover the range of scores on a 1–5 scoring scale.

As important as seeing the sample essays and their scores is understanding *why* they received the scores that they did. A detailed assessment of each essay is provided to help you see why it earned that particular score. Read each sample essay and its assessment carefully. If you have difficulty understanding why the essay received its score, take another look at the scoring chart printed on pages 170–171 in the answer key.

The first sample essay exam assignment is modeled after the SAT II Writing Test. The second is similar to an exam you might be given in an English course and deals with a specific literary text, *Frankenstein*.

SAMPLE ESSAY EXAM #1

Assignment:

"Problems are opportunities in disguise." Write an essay in which you agree or disagree with this statement. Use an example from your personal experience, current events, history, literature, or another discipline to support your answer. Do not write on any other topic. Essays on other topics will not be considered. Use the space below to write your answer.

Time allowed: 20 minutes

SAMPLE ESSAY RESPONSE #1

Drip, drip, drip. The puddle of water on the floor just kept getting bigger and bigger. Where was our landlord when we needed him? He was out of town—for a whole week. But with all that goes on in our apartment, we couldn't wait until he got back to fix the leak in our kitchen sink, and my mom couldn't afford a couple hundred dollars to pay for a plummer on her own. We certainly had a problem on our hands. But, like most problems, it turned out to be a wonderful opportunity in disguise.

I've learned that problems are opportunities from watching my mother. A single mother of seven, she tackles life's problems (and believe me, we have plenty) with a positive attitude. She has taught me that each problem presents a unique opportunity to learn something new about myself or the world around me.

My mom's solution to this problem, was to wash all the dishes in the bathroom sink and wait a few days until our Uncle Albert could come over and fix the kitchen sink. "It'll give me a few days to clean all the junk out from underneath the sink, anyway," she said. But I had a better idea. Without telling my mom, I went to the library. I found a great fix-it-yourself book, and in just a few hours, I had figured out how to fix the leak.

I hurried home and borrowed some tools from our neighbor. With my little brother as my assistant, I went to work. By the time my mom got home that night, I had the sink fixed, and my sister Angela had just about finished cleaning up the mess underneath so my mother wouldn't have to.

With all the cooking and cleaning that we have to do, that leaky sink could have been a minor disaster in our busy apartment. Instead, it became a chance for me to learn something new—and a chance to make life easier for my whole family. Further, I learned a skill that I'll be able to use throughout my lifetime. For once, I'm *glad* our landlord wasn't around when we needed him.

Assessment

On a scale of 1–5, this essay is a 5.

- The essay fully meets the requirements of the assignment.
- The introduction catches the reader's attention.
- The thesis is strong and stated clearly.
- The writer provides a solid supporting example.

- The writer offers details and descriptions that bring the example to life.
- There are strong transitions within and between paragraphs.
- The conclusion offers a new understanding and provides a sense of closure; it also frames the essay.
- Individual sentences are strong and clear, and there is good variety in sentence structure.
- The writer uses stylistic devices and punctuation for special effect (for example, "Drip, drip, drip").
- The essay is nearly error-free; there is only one spelling mistake (plummer) and one misplaced comma.

SAMPLE ESSAY RESPONSE #2

Just the word "problem" can send people into a panic. But problems can be good things, too. Problems are situations, that make us think and to be creative and resourcefull. They can also teach us things we didn't know before.

For example, I had a problem in school a few years ago when I couldn't understand my math class. I was failing quizzes and homeworks. I wasn't sure what to do. I went to the teacher and asked for help. She says she'll set me up to be tutored by another student. But I have to help that student around school. I wasn't sure what she meant by that. Until I met my tutor. She was handicaped and had a disability.

My job was to help her carry her books from class-to-class. I'd never even spoken to someone in a wheel-chair before, I was a little scared. But she turned out to be really great and I did better in math, to.

So you see that wonderful things can come out of problems. You just have to remember to look for the positive things and not focus on the negative.

Assessment

On a scale of 1–5, this essay is a 3.

- The essay meets the requirements of the assignment, but not strongly.
- The writer clearly states her thesis, but support for that thesis is weak.
- The writer defines "problem," but not quite accurately.
- The essay starts to develop an example, but not sufficiently. Many assertions are left unsupported. For example, what made her tutor "really great"?
- The main example doesn't quite support the thesis. How did this problem challenge her to be resourceful and creative? What did it teach her that she didn't know before?
- The essay lacks detail and description and uses mostly general words instead of specific and exact words.
- The essay is occasionally repetitive (for example, "handicapped and disabled").
- While there is some sentence variety, most sentences follow the same basic pattern.
- There are several sentence fragments, run-ons, and misspelled words as well as a shift in tense.
- The conclusion is abrupt.

SAMPLE ESSAY RESPONSE #3

I agree with the quote that problems are opportunities in disguise. Sometimes problems, are opportunities, to.

I have a lot of problems like anyone else does. Sometimes there very difficult and I don't no how to handle them. When I have a relly big problem, sometimes ask my parents or friend's for advise. Sometimes they help, sometimes they don't, then I have to figure out how to handle it myself.

One time I had a big problem. Where someone stole my wallet. I had to get to a job interview. But I had no money and no ID. I was so upset. This happened in school. So I went to the princaples office and reported it. He called the man I was suppose to interview with. Who rescheduled the interview for me. So I still had the opportunity to interview and I'm proud to say I got the job. But I quit a few weeks later, I didn't like it very much. Now I have a better job.

In conclusion; problems can be opportunities in disguise if you just look at them that way. Instead of the other way around.

Assessment

On a scale of 1–5, this essay ranks a 2.

- The essay states a thesis that responds to the assignment, but it does not support that thesis.
- The introduction does not try to grab a reader's attention and is repetitive.
- The second paragraph is mostly "filler"—it talks about problems in general and does not address the thesis.
- The third paragraph offers an example of a problem the writer faced, but it does not explain how that problem was an opportunity in disguise. (There's no new opportunity that came out if it; he was going to have his interview before he had the problem anyway.)
- The essay lacks focus. Notice how the third paragraph starts to develop a new topic—the writer's job.
- The conclusion could be offering a new understanding, but it is unclear what "instead of the other way around" means.
- There are a lot of simple sentences with the same basic sentence pattern.
- The writer relies on general words and does not provide any detail or description.
- The writer also relies on the tired phrase "in conclusion."
- There are sentence fragments, run-ons, and other grammatical problems throughout the essay.
- There are numerous spelling and punctuation errors.

SAMPLE ESSAY EXAM #2

Assignment: Please answer the following question in a well-developed essay. Be sure your essay has a clear thesis and that you provide sufficient evidence for that thesis from the text.

In the novel *Frankenstein*, who is more of a monster: Victor Frankenstein or his creature? Why do you think so?

Time allowed: 45 minutes

SAMPLE ESSAY RESPONSE #1

In *Frankenstien*, the creature commits several murders. He kills Frankenstein's brother, best friend, father, and wife—the four people Frankenstein loved most in the world. For this reason, many people think that the creature is a monster. But he's not the real monster in the novel. The real monster is his creator Victor Frankenstien.

In the novel, the creature only kills because he has been treated so badly by his creator and everyone else who he meets. Because the creature is so ugly, everyone assumes that he is a monster. They run from him, throw things at him, curse him, they even shoot him after he saves a little girl from drowning. Why shouldn't he hate mankind if he has only known hatred? The real reason he only knows hatred is because Victor Frankenstien abandoned him. Frankenstien is responsible for these murders, not his poor creature.

The creature is like a child, he only wants to be loved. Maybe he could handle everyone else hating him if he were loved by his "father." But even his father Frankenstien rejects him. In fact Frankenstien rejected him the moment he was "born." He ran away from the creature, who didn't know where (or what) he was. He didn't even know how to speak or talk. And then, to make matters worse, Frankenstein doesn't tell anyone about the creature. So no one knows to beware of the monster.

Frankenstien doesn't tell anyone even after three people are dead. He could have prevented their deaths. If he hadn't been so selfish. He keeps his secret because he doesn't want people to hate him for creating and letting lose a monster. But he doesn't realize that the creature wouldn't have become a monster in the first place if Frankenstien wouldn't have treated him so badly.

Frankenstien is also more of a monster for another reason. He destroys the "bride" he was creating for the creature, tearing her up right in front of the poor creature's eyes.

Frankenstien is clearly more of a monster than his creature. The creature helped keep the DeLaceys from starving, saved the little girl from drowning. He wanted to love and be loved. But all he got was rejection and hatred. And for that, only Frankenstien is to blame.

Assessment

On a scale of 1–5, this essay ranks a 4.

- The essay completely fulfills the assignment.
- The thesis is clear and assertive.
- The essay offers several ideas to support the thesis. Three of the supporting paragraphs are strong, but the fourth (about Frankenstein's destruction of the creature's "bride") is insufficiently developed.
- The essay addresses a key counterargument in the first paragraph, but there are several other counterarguments that probably should also be addressed (for example, Frankenstein has several logical reasons for abandoning the creation of the creature's "bride").
- The introduction is not particularly catchy, but it provides necessary context.
- The writer makes good use of parallel structure (in the second and eighth sentences) and there is good sentence variety throughout.
- There is some effective word choice ("abandon," "beware") but some words are repeated rather frequently.

- There are inconsistencies in verb tense and a few run-ons and fragments, but most sentences are grammatically correct and clear.
- There are a few mechanical errors, including the misspelling of Frankenstein, but they do not interfere with clear expression of ideas.

SAMPLE ESSAY RESPONSE #2

In Frankenstine, who is the monster? Is it the creature. Or is it the creator of the creature, Victor Frankenstine. It is a good question. One that has many possible answers. In my opinion, I think Mary Shelly was trying to make us wonder about monsters. The creature looks like a monster, he is big and ugly. Everyone is afraid of him, even Frankenstine. He's like the monsters are nightmares in our dreams. Frankenstine made him one nite out of pieces of dead people. He was a graverobber. Frankenstine never tells how he actually begot the creature to live. That was frustrating. Also there are many parts of the story that are hard to follow. I didn't like it very much. I don't like how the creature kills so many people. And gets away with it. What confused me is who is Walton? At the end of the story he sees the creature on the boat and he tries to kill him but he kills himself instead.

Assessment

On a scale of 1–5, this essay ranks a 1.

- The essay does not fulfill the requirements of the assignment. It never answers the question of who is more of a monster. It only *repeats* the question and then changes the subject.
- There does not appear to be a thesis.
- The essay lacks focus. In its single paragraph, the essay brings up several different ideas without relating them to each other or to one controlling idea.
- None of the ideas raised in that paragraph are sufficiently developed. There are no supporting ideas or examples (with the possible exception of the seventh sentence).
- The paragraph spends most of its time summarizing and asking questions rather than analyzing the issue.
- The first part of the essay is mostly "fluff"—empty sentences that avoid taking a stand on the issue.
- The essay contains wordiness and unnecessary repetition.
- There are several unclear pronoun references in the last part of the essay, creating confusion (who tries to kill whom? who commits suicide?).
- The essay relies on general rather than specific and exact words.
- There are numerous grammatical and mechanical errors throughout the essay, including fragments, run-ons, incorrect punctuation, and misspelled words.

PRACTICE

Assess the essay you wrote for the practice exercise in Lesson 19. On a scale of 1–5, how would you rate your essay? What are its strengths? What are its weaknesses? Identify the things you did well in your essay. Then, list the ways you think your essay could be improved.

CONGRATULATIONS!

You've completed 20 lessons and have learned a great deal about how to write more effective essays. To see just how much you've learned, turn the page and take the Post-Test. You should see a dramatic improvement in your understanding of the writing process and in your ability to write clearly and effectively in an essay format.

To keep your writing skills sharp, write regularly. Start a journal, write letters to friends, take a composition class, or join a writer's group. You don't have to write only essays to practice communicating clearly. And the more you practice, the easier it will be for you to express yourself in writing. Meanwhile, reward yourself for a job well done!

POST-TEST

I f you'd like to gauge how much your essay writing skills and your understanding of the writing process have improved from your work in this book, take the following post-test. Though the questions are different from the pretest, the format is the same, so you will be able to directly compare test results.

When you complete this test, check your answers, and then compare your score with the score you received on the pretest. If your score is much higher than your pretest score, congratulations—you've profited noticeably from your hard work. If your score shows little improvement, perhaps there are certain chapters you should review. Whatever your score on this post-test, keep this book around for review and refer to it whenever you need tips on the essay writing process.

You can use the space on the pages following Part II of the post-test to record your answers. Or, if you prefer, simply circle the answers directly for Part I. If this book doesn't belong to you, don't write in the book. Write the numbers 1–20 on a piece of paper and record your answers there. Use a sheet of loose-leaf or other $8\frac{1}{2} \times 11$ ruled paper for your essay.

You can take as much time as you need for Part I, though it probably shouldn't take you more than 20 minutes. When you've finished, check your answers against the answer key at the end of the book. Once again, the answer key indicates which lesson addresses the key concept in each question. Set aside another 30 minutes to complete Part II.

Good luck!

PART I

1. If your essay is very well written, it's okay not to completely fulfill the assignment.

   a. true
   b. false

2. In general, you should write for which audience?

   a. your classmates
   b. your teacher, admissions counselor, or exam reader
   c. yourself
   d. a general reader

3. Which of the following introductory tasks does the introduction below fail to do?

   In this essay, I would like to consider why the United States dropped the atomic bomb on Hiroshima at the end of World War II. Some people contend it was necessary to end the war. However, there is considerable evidence that suggests we could have won the war without the bomb. More importantly, that evidence suggests that our decision to drop the bomb was political, not military.

   a. provide context
   b. state the thesis
   c. grab the reader's attention
   d. set the tone for the essay

4. In the paragraph below, which sentence is the topic sentence?

   Too much sun can be deadly. First of all, too much sun can dry your skin, which in turn reduces its elasticity and speeds the aging process. Second, too much sun can burn unprotected skin and cause permanent discoloration and damage to the dermis. Most importantly, long-term exposure of unprotected skin can result in skin cancer.

   a. the first sentence
   b. the second sentence
   c. the third sentence
   d. the fourth sentence

5. Which two organizational strategies does the paragraph above use?

   a. order of importance and comparison/contrast
   b. cause/effect and chronology
   c. classification and chronology
   d. order of importance and cause/effect

6. Three supporting ideas should be sufficient for any essay assignment.

   a. true

   b. false

7. A single-sentence paragraph is appropriate if:

   a. you don't have any support for the assertion in that sentence

   b. you have too many long paragraphs throughout the essay

   c. it's a particularly well-written sentence

   d. you really want to emphasize the idea in that sentence

8. Read the following essay assignment carefully. Which of the sentences below best describes the kind of essay that you should write?

In Civilization and Its Discontents, *Freud explains why he believes civilized people are unhappy. Summarize his theory and evaluate it.*

   a. Describe the main points of Freud's theory and assess the validity of that theory.

   b. Define "civilization" and show examples of civilized communities.

   c. Describe several examples that illustrate Freud's theory.

   d. Describe the main points of Freud's theory and express your opinion about his theory.

9. When revising an essay, which of the following issues should you address first?

   a. grammar and spelling

   b. organization and transitions

   c. thesis and support

   d. introductory paragraph

10. Which sentence below has the most effective word choice?

   a. She was scared.

   b. She was petrified.

   c. She was frightened.

   d. She was scared stiff.

11. Which of the following would be a problem in a concluding paragraph?

   a. it doesn't restate the thesis

   b. it doesn't frame the essay

   c. it arouses the reader's emotions

   d. it doesn't bring up any ideas that aren't related to the thesis

12. Which of the following is typically the best organizational strategy in an argument?

    a. order of importance (least to most important)

    b. order of importance (most to least important)

    c. cause and effect

    d. comparison and contrast

13. Identify the grammatical problem in the following sentence:

After he mastered the trumpet, he learned how to play the piano, and then he goes on to become one of the greatest jazz pianists in the world.

    a. sentence fragment

    b. run-on sentence

    c. inconsistent verb tense

    d. parallelism

14. On an essay exam, most of your time should be spent:

    a. planning

    b. drafting

    c. revising

    d. editing

15. An introduction should never be more than one paragraph long.

    a. true

    b. false

16. What is the main problem with the following sentence?

After his fight with Alan, he swore he would never let anyone use his car again without his permission.

    a. It's a run-on sentence.

    b. It's not properly punctuated.

    c. It's unnecessarily wordy.

    d. Its pronouns may be confusing.

17. A thesis should be which of the following?

    a. short

    b. clear

    c. assertive

    d. (a) and (b)

    e. (b) and (c)

18. Outlining should typically take place:

a. before you brainstorm

b. after you brainstorm

c. after your first rough draft

d. after you gloss

19. Which of the underlined words in the following paragraph are transitions?

Too much(1) *sun can be deadly.* *First of all*(2), *too much sun can dry your skin, which in turn reduces its elasticity* *and*(3) *speeds the aging process.* *Second*(4), *too much sun can burn unprotected skin and cause permanent discoloration and damage* *to the dermis*(5). *Most importantly*(6), *long-term exposure of unprotected skin* *can result in*(7) *skin cancer.*

a. (1), (2) and (3)

b. (2), (4) and (5)

c. (2), (6) and (7)

d. (2), (4) and (6)

20. Credibility is established by which of the following:

a. expertise and freedom from bias

b. expertise and education

c. education and bias

d. reputation, accomplishments, and freedom from bias

PART II

Set a timer for 30 minutes. When you're ready to begin, read the essay assignment below carefully. Use the space below to write your essay. STOP writing when 30 minutes have passed, even if you haven't completed your essay. When you've finished, look at the scoring chart in the answer key at the end of the book to estimate your essay's grade.

ESSAY ASSIGNMENT

Many people feel that a movie isn't a true success if it doesn't force viewers to think about an important issue or idea. Others argue that movies are successful so long as they entertain us; they don't have to have any ideological, political, or social agenda. What do you think? Is it enough that a movie is entertaining? Or should it do more? Why? Provide specific examples to support your position.

ANSWERS AND EXPLANATIONS

This section provides answers, sample answers, and explanations for the pretest, the practice exercises, and the post-test. Please keep in mind that most of the practice exercises ask you to do your own writing, so each answer will be unique. Use the answers and explanations as guides to help assess your understanding of the lessons.

PRETEST

PART I

If you miss any of the answers, you can find help for that kind of question in the lesson(s) shown to the right of the answer.

Question	Answer	Lesson
1	b	11
2	c	8, 12
3	d	12
4	a	1
5	a	16
6	d	6, 7
7	b	2
8	c	6
9	b	5, 8

Question	Answer	Lesson
10	b	9
11	c	10
12	a	13
13	d	15
14	c	18
15	a	3, 4
16	b	14-17
17	e	10
18	b	9, 15
19	c	16
20	d	11

PART II

Use the Scoring Chart below to evaluate your essay. First, score your essay yourself and then find someone else (an English teacher or a friend who has strong writing skills) to score your essay as well. After you assign a number for each of the categories shown on the scoring chart, average the numbers to get an overall score.

Characteristic	5	4	3	2	1
Response to Assignment	Completely fulfills the assignment; may go beyond the requirements to a new level.	Fulfills all of the requirements of the assignment.	Fulfills most of the requirements of the assignment.	Fails to fulfill a major part of the assignment.	Does not fulfill the assignment.
Thesis	Is clear, assertive, and original.	Is clear and assertive.	Is suggested but may be weak or unclear.	Is weak and/or unclear.	No recognizable thesis.
Development	Several strong supporting ideas are offered; each idea is thoroughly developed.	Several supporting ideas are offered; most are adequately developed, but one or two are underdeveloped.	Offers some supporting ideas but not enough to make a strong case; ideas may be underdeveloped.	Few supporting ideas are offered; the ideas that are provided are insufficiently developed.	Little or no support is offered; ideas are poorly developed.
Focus	All ideas are directly and clearly related to the thesis.	Most ideas are directly and clearly related to the thesis.	A majority of ideas are related but there are some loose connections and/or digressions.	Some focus, but many ideas are unrelated.	No focus; most ideas are unrelated to the thesis or topic.

Characteristic	5	4	3	2	1
Argumentation	Addresses counterarguments, makes concessions, and establishes credibility.	Addresses most counterarguments, establishes credibility for most sources; may neglect to make concessions.	Addresses some counterarguments but may neglect some major counterpoints; establishes credibility for some sources.	Fails to address most counterarguments; does not establish credibility for most sources; does not make concessions.	Does not address counterarguments, establish credibility, or make concessions.
Organization	Ideas are well organized; structure is clear; provides strong transitions throughout.	Ideas are well organized; good transitions throughout most of essay.	Essay has organizing principle but pattern may be disrupted; some ideas are out of order; some transitions may be weak or missing.	Organizing principle may be unclear; many transitions are missing.	No organizing principle; weak or missing transitions throughout the essay.
Sentences	Ideas come across clearly; variety in sentence structure.	Most ideas are clear; may occasionally be wordy.	Sentences may be cluttered with unnecessary words or repetition; ambiguity may interfere with clarity.	Sentences are often wordy or ambiguous, interfering with clarity.	A majority of sentences are wordy or ambiguous, often interfering with clarity.
Word Choice	Precise and careful word choice; avoids jargon and pretentious language.	Most words are exact and appropriate; an occasionally ineffective word choice.	Mix of general and specific words; some pretentious language or jargon.	Mostly general, inexact words; word choice sometimes inappropriate.	Word choice often ineffective or inappropriate.
Grammar	Virtually error free.	A few grammatical errors, but none that interfere with clarity.	Several grammatical errors; may interfere with clarity.	Many grammatical errors; often interfere with clarity.	Most sentences have grammatical errors, often interfering with clarity.
Mechanics	Virtually error free.	A few mechanical errors, but none that interfere with clarity.	Several mechanical errors; some may interfere with clarity.	Many mechanical errors that interfere with clarity.	Most sentences have mechanical errors that interfere with clarity.

LESSON 1

PRACTICE 1

1. The "actual reader" is the person or people who will actually be reading your essay—your instructor, the college admissions counselor, the AP or SAT II exam evaluator. The "general reader" is the audience most actual readers want you to write for. This reader is the "average" person, someone who may or may not know anything about you or your subject matter, so you need to carefully consider what your reader may or may not know and provide the appropriate context.

2. (a) In this case, you have been given a specific audience to write for: a Martian. You are not writing for a general reader.

   (b) Since your audience is a Martian, you can assume that he has very little knowledge of America. He may not have any knowledge of the concept of democracy, for example, or of freedom of speech. In fact, he many not even know what you mean by "country" or "nation." For this assignment, you will have to explain all of your terms carefully and not take anything for granted.

PRACTICE 2

Answers will vary. Here are two possibilities:

   Assignment 1: My goal is to demonstrate the truth of Melville's quote. I'll use the time I got lost in New York City as my example.

   Assignment 2: My goal is to explain the conflict that Hughes felt and show how he resolved that conflict.

LESSON 2

PRACTICE 1

1.

Subject	Directions
the change in citizens' attitudes towards the presidency in the last decade	describe
what I think caused this change	explain
the impact of this attitude on the power of the president	assess

2.

Subject	Directions
whether Charity Royall has control over her destiny	answer and explain

3.

Subject	Directions
the Paracelsian cosmos	describe
similarities between Paracelsian and Aristotelian cosmos	compare
differences between Paracelsian and Aristotelian cosmos	contrast
connection of Paracelsus' notion of disease to his cosmology	explain
differences between Paracelsus' notion of disease and Galen's notion	contrast

PRACTICE 2

Answers will vary slightly.

1. Tell what citizens' attitudes toward the presidency used to be and what they are now; tell what I think caused this change and why; and explain how I think this attitude has affected the power of the presidency.

2. Tell whether I think Charity has control over her destiny and why I think so, using examples from the novel to support my answer.

3. Tell readers what the Paracelsian cosmos is like, including how it is similar to, and different from, the Aristotelian cosmos; show how Paracelsus' notion of disease is connected to his cosmology; and show the differences between Paracelsus' and Galen's notions of disease.

LESSON 3

PRACTICE 1

Answers will vary. Here's one possibility:

When I was in ninth grade, it was chemistry class, the first exam, and a lot of people were cheating—I mean *a lot*. They all had cheat sheets and were even passing them back and forth. I was still pretty new to the school, and I had made some friends but wasn't really close with anyone in the class, and I had studied really, really hard for the exam. I was really angry. And I couldn't believe the teacher didn't notice it. She looked up once or twice but didn't seem to see a thing. I was having trouble with one of the problems and thought about cheating, too, but of course I hadn't prepared a cheat sheet like everyone else. I knew that if I told on the cheaters, it could mean real trouble for me. I was new to the school and that was hard enough. I really didn't want to be an outcast. So after the test, I left an anonymous note for the teacher. I typed it and slipped it onto her desk when no one was around. I was really worried someone would catch me in the act. When Ms. Waller confronted the class, it was so tense! I could see the cheaters looking around trying to figure out who told. I guess being new was lucky for me because no one really suspected me of tattling. But then they started to blame Pearl. And boy were they mean to her. They wrote stuff on her locker, knocked her books out of her hand, tripped her in the hallway. That kind of stuff really gets to you. I was so upset. If I told them

I did it, then they'd do the same to me. But I felt really bad about it. She got picked on enough as it was. So finally I confessed to Rob. He cheated with the others but he left Pearl alone. I asked him not to tell the others it was me but to ask them to leave Pearl alone. He did, but then they harassed him until he told them it was me. What a mess. I'll never forget that day at school when I found out they knew. (Maybe I could start the essay by describing that day.) Someone actually threw food at me in the cafeteria. I guess it worked out ok, because they'd already gotten it out of their system with Pearl, but the name "Rat" stuck with me for a long time, and I had a tough time fitting in. A lot of people didn't want to be friends with me that year. Even Pearl was mad because I waited so long to tell the truth. I don't know if I'd do the same thing again. It was really painful. It's so hard to fit in and do what's right!

PRACTICE 2
Again, answers will vary. Here's one possibility:

A strong determining factor for my sense of identity: Being Vietnamese-American
- speaking one language at home and in the neighborhood, another at school
- not being able to express myself all the time with my American friends
- my parents being mad when I forget how to say something in Vietnamese
- having to serve as a translator for my parents
- my accent
- real difficulty at first reading English
- shyness, especially in the classroom
- people assuming I don't speak English
- people assuming other things, like that I always eat rice
- feeling more comfortable with other "hyphenated Americans"
- feeling most comfortable with other Vietnamese-Americans

LESSON 4

PRACTICE 1
Answers will vary. Here's one possibility:

- What are the benefits of school uniforms?
- Who would decide what students would wear?
- Who would pay for uniforms?
- What about families that can't afford uniforms?
- Would uniforms actually save poor families money (fewer clothes to buy)?
- How would the policy be enforced?
- What about accessories, like jewelry, and belts? Would they be regulated?

- Would there be special days to wear whatever you like?
- Do uniforms create a sense of community?
- Would students be angry?
- How long would they stay angry?
- What if you didn't like the colors, or you felt that the uniform made you look ugly or fat?
- How many public schools require uniforms?
- How successful have they been?
- How do students feel? Would they go back to freedom of dress?
- Does it improve discipline? How?

PRACTICE 2

Again, answers will vary. Please see the example on page 36 in Lesson 4.

LESSON 5

PRACTICE 1

Answers will vary. Here's one possibility:

Assignment:	Identify a factor that you believe figures strongly in a child's personality development. Explain how that factor may influence the child.
Broad topic:	Factors influencing a child's personality development
Narrowed topic:	Parents
Further narrowed topic:	Parents who have to work
Sufficiently narrowed topic:	What kind of child care parents choose for their children
Topic turned into a question:	How does the kind of child care working parents choose affect a child's personality development?
Tentative thesis:	The kind of child care working parents choose has a powerful impact on a child's personality development.

PRACTICE 2

Again, answers will vary. Here's one possibility:

Assignment:	Discuss how religion influences culture. Use specific examples from the religions we've studied so far.
Broad topic:	How religion influences culture.
Narrowed topic:	How religion influences laws.
Sufficiently narrowed topic:	How Islamic and Christian beliefs shaped laws in the Middle East and Europe.

Topic turned into a question:	How have Islamic and Christian beliefs shaped the laws in the Middle East and Europe?
Tentative thesis:	The laws in the Middle East are based on the Koran, while the laws in Europe have their basis in the Bible, particularly the Ten Commandments.

LESSON 6

PRACTICE 1

Answers will vary. Here's a chronological outline for the freewriting exercise in Lesson 3:

1. Studied all week to get ready for exam.
2. Taking the exam—seeing everyone cheating. Very angry.
3. Typing up note at home.
4. Sneaking into classroom to leave note for teacher.
5. Teacher confronting class.
6. People deciding it was Pearl who told on them.
7. Being mean to Pearl.
8. Trying to decide what to do.
   explaining situation to friends in chat room
   deciding had to take blame off of Pearl
9. Telling Rob.
10. Walking into cafeteria and having people make fun of me.
    finding out Rob told everyone
11. People avoiding me for weeks.

PRACTICE 2

Answers will vary. Here's an outline for the same freewriting exercise using cause and effect as the main organizing principle:

How I came to be called "The Rat":
1. Start with walking into the cafeteria and people pointing at me, saying, "Look, there's the Rat!"
2. Describe how I'd left an anonymous note for the teacher
   ■ Describe why—the test
3. Describe how Pearl was blamed
4. Describe dilemma—wanting to take blame off Pearl but not wanting to be hated by the others
5. Talk about consequences of doing what I thought was right:
   ■ Nickname
   ■ People avoiding me

6. Describe how I feel about it now
   - Still think I did the right thing, but should have given my name from the beginning
   - My fear of being outcast made me give an anonymous note; that way the teacher couldn't help Pearl, or me, until it was too late
   - Learned that if I think something is right (or wrong), I should stand up for it (or against it) totally, not just halfway.

LESSON 7

PRACTICE 1

Answers will vary. Here's an outline using order of importance for the school uniforms issue:

School uniforms: a good idea
1. Students and parents will save time and money.
   - spend less time worrying about what to wear
   - spend less time shopping
   - spend less money on clothes (fewer clothes needed)
2. Students will be more confident.
   - will equalize students who can afford the most stylish or expensive clothes with those who can't
   - will take the focus away from appearance so students can focus more on schoolwork
     - with more focus on work, students will do better in school
   - will help students feel like they belong.
     - Students need to feel like they belong to feel good about themselves
     - Uniforms help create a sense of community and belonging.
3. Students will be better disciplined.
   - Uniforms create a tone of seriousness.
   - Uniforms make it easier to focus on schoolwork.

PRACTICE 2

Answers will vary. Here's part of an outline using comparison and contrast for the child care issue.

Two options: nanny or day care
1. One caregiver vs. many
   a. with nanny, child has one primary caregiver
      (i) develops strong bond with one person
      (ii) develops deep feeling of trust and security
   b. with day care, child has several caregivers
      (i) more difficult to develop strong bond with one person

2. One child vs. many
   a. with nanny, child gets great deal of individual attention (even if there are siblings)
     (i) all of child's needs are attended to
   b. with day care, child competes for attention with other children
     (i) some of child's needs may not be attended to, or at least not immediately
     (ii) child will develop social skills more rapidly by being in company of other children

LESSON 8

PRACTICE 1

Answers will vary. Here's one possibility:

I never spend much time planning my essay. A lot of times I procrastinate and wait until the day before the paper is due to get started—especially if I don't like the assignment. Then I'll just sit down and write a draft. Sometimes I get stuck for a long time on the introduction. I have to have my introduction done before I write the body of an essay. Sometimes I get stuck too because I have trouble organizing my ideas. I usually don't outline unless my teacher says I have to. I should start doing outlines (at least rough ones) and start working on my essays earlier. I also need to make sure I am clearer about my audience and purpose. I think I'd write better (and be more relaxed) if I did some brainstorming as soon as I got the assignment, then drafted a thesis and outline, and *then* wrote a draft.

PRACTICE 2

Answers will vary. Here are some possibilities:

1. Briarwood offers everything I'm looking for in a college: a renowned child psychology program; a small, beautiful campus not too far from home; and opportunities to develop my leadership skills through extracurricular programs.

2. Because innocent people can be (and have been) killed, the death penalty should be abolished.

3. Ever since I read *The Grapes of Wrath*, I have been fascinated by American history.

4. The Internet must remain a completely uncensored environment.

PRACTICE 3

Answers will vary. Here are two examples:

1. Doing what was right was more difficult than I'd ever imagined.

2. Uniforms for public school students will benefit everyone: parents, teachers, and most importantly, children.

LESSON 9

PRACTICE 1

Though answers may vary, the most logical way to divide this text into paragraphs is probably the following. Notice that each of the three parts of the personality gets its own paragraph. The topic sentence in each of those paragraphs describes the main characteristic of that part of the personality:

Sigmund Freud, the father of psychoanalysis, made many contributions to the science of psychology. One of his greatest contributions was his theory of the personality. <u>According to Freud, the human personality is made up of three parts: the id, the ego, and the superego.</u>

<u>The id is the part of the personality that exists only in the subconscious.</u> *According to Freud, the id has no direct contact with reality. It is the innermost core of our personality and operates according to the pleasure principle. That is, it seeks immediate gratification for its desires, regardless of eternal realities or consequences. It is not even aware that external realities or consequences exist.*

<u>The ego develops from the id and is the part of the personality in contact with the real world.</u> *The ego is conscious and therefore aims to satisfy the subconscious desires of the id as best it can within the individual's environment. When it can't satisfy those desires, it tries to control or suppress the id. The ego functions according to the reality principle.*

The superego is the third and final part of the personality to develop. <u>This is the part of the personality that contains our moral values and ideals, our notion of what's right and wrong.</u> *The superego gives us the "rules" that help the ego control the id. For example, a child wants a toy that belongs to another child (id). He checks his environment to see if it's possible to take that toy (ego). He can, and does. But then he remembers that it's wrong to take something that belongs to someone else (superego) and returns the toy to the other child.*

PRACTICE 2

Answers will vary. The topic sentences are boldfaced below.

1. **The demand for health care workers is on the rise.** The government's Bureau of Labor Statistics (BLS) reports that employment in health service industries through the year 2005 will grow at almost double the rate of all other (non-farm) wage and salary employment. In sheer numbers, about 9 million American workers are now employed in health services. By 2005, that number is expected to be at about 13 million—an increase of nearly 4 million jobs.

2. When I was in kindergarten, I wanted to be an astronaut. When I was in junior high school, I wanted to be a doctor. When I was in high school, I wanted to be a teacher. Today, I'm 35 and I'm a firefighter. **I'm none of the things I thought I wanted to be—and I couldn't be happier.**

3. **While the proposed tax referendum sounds good, it's actually bad news for most citizens of Algonquin County.** It will not reduce taxes for middle income families. In fact, middle income families with children will pay 10 percent *more* per year, and families without children will pay 20 percent more. Further, the referendum actually *decreases* taxes for the wealthiest tax bracket. In fact, taxpayers in the highest income bracket will pay 10 percent less per year if the referendum is passed.

LESSON 10

PRACTICE 1 and 2

Answers will vary. If you take another look at the outline for school uniforms (see the answer section for Lesson 7), you can see how each of the three main supporting ideas has several supporting ideas of its own. Below you'll find additional support for one of those ideas. Notice the mix of specific examples, facts, reasons, descriptions, and expert opinion.

- Students will be more confident.
    - will equalize students who can afford the most stylish or expensive clothes with those who can't
    - Students often judge each other based on dress.
- The most popular kids are usually the ones who can also keep up with the most recent fashion trends. "In any school yard, all you have to do is look around to see how important clothing is in defining groups and determining social status. The most popular students are always the ones in the designer clothes. The least popular are often dressed in clothes that are two, three or more fashion cycles out of date." Edward Jones, "The Clothes Make the Kid," *American View* magazine.
- Status is often determined by how you dress, not who you are.
    - A shirt that says Calvin Klein or Tommy Hilfager isn't just a shirt; it's a status symbol.
    - "A student who wears 'retro' clothing will often be seen as 'cool' or 'hip' while someone who wears polyester trousers and a pocket protector will be stereotyped as a 'nerd' or a 'dork'—even though he may be just as 'hip' as she."—Jamie Ernstein, professor of cultural studies, personal interview.
- Logos and labels have now become part of the design in clothing. A t-shirt that used to have a picture or geometric design will now sport the company's logo—Gap, Old Navy, Guess, and so on.
- If everyone has to wear uniforms, the social divisions created by those who can afford designer clothing and those who can't will disappear.
- Students will be judged for who they are again, not for what they wear.

LESSON 11

PRACTICE 1

Answers will vary. Here are two sample profiles and sentences that establish each source's credibility:

Fact 1: The average television channel shows 579 acts of violence in a 24-hour period.

Source: Emily Rhodes

Profile: Professor of Communication, New Jersey State University

Founder, American Society for Media Responsibility

Author of four books on the relationship between television and violence

Sentence: According to Emily Rhodes, professor of communication at New Jersey State University and author of four books on the relationship between television and violence, the average television channel shows 579 acts of violence in a 24-hour period.

Fact 2: Violent crimes committed by juveniles have quadrupled since 1973.

Source: Children's Watch

Profile: Nonprofit organization

Studies children's issues, including crime, child labor, abuse, and so on.

Affiliated with New York State University

Their annual report, "The State of Our Children," is required reading for UN, WHO, and governmental policy makers

Sentence: Children's Watch, a nonprofit dedicated to researching children's issues, claims that the number of violent crimes committed by juveniles has quadrupled since 1973—a fact that won't be overlooked by the government, since the group's annual report, "The State of Our Children," is required reading for members of both the House of Representatives and the Senate.

PRACTICE 2

Answers will vary. Here's one possibility:

Thesis: Despite the dangers, the Internet should remain a totally free and uncensored medium.

Supporting Points:
- Censorship would violate the right to free speech.
- Censorship of material on the Internet could set a precedent for censorship in other media.
- The courts would be clogged with cases regarding censorship because the definition of whatever material should be censored would necessarily be vague and subject to interpretation.

The Opposition's Position:
- Hate speech—when it incites violence—does not fall under protection of the First Amendment.

- Nudity, cursing, and violence are limited on television, which kids can access 24-hours a day. How is the Internet different? Kids can access it 24-hours a day, too, with no one to control which sites they visit.
- Determining what kind of material should be censored will lead to a nationwide examination of our values.

Paragraph Acknowledging the Opposition:

First and foremost, censorship on the Internet violates one of the principles upon which this country was founded: freedom of speech. It is true that some sites present lewd or hateful images and ideas, but this kind of hate speech can be found anywhere, in all kinds of publications and all kinds of media. The Internet just makes it easier for people to find this information. If someone really wants to commit an act of violence, a Web site isn't what's going to push him or her into committing a hate crime.

LESSON 12

PRACTICE 1

Answers will vary, of course. Here's an introduction to the school uniforms essay that uses surprising facts to catch the reader's attention:

> At Jamestown Senior High School, an amazing thing happened. In just one year, student thefts dropped from 58 to 18; assaults plunged from 32 to 5; and total disciplinary actions plummeted from 112 to 42. The dramatic change at Jamestown High was created by the institution of a simple policy, one that should be instituted at middle and high schools nationwide: school uniforms.

PRACTICE 2

Here's another introduction for the school uniforms essay, this time using an anecdote:

> Paula always wore the same two or three outfits. She decided she'd rather be made fun of for wearing the same clothes all the time than for wearing the cheap, no-name gear that made up most of her wardrobe. At least these outfits gave her a shot at hanging out with the cool kids. At least she could proudly display the Calvin Klein, DKNY, and Guess logos.
>
> Unfortunately, Paula's attitude toward clothing is all too common among students who spend more time worrying about what they (and others) are wearing than about what they're supposed to be learning. School uniforms can help change that—and help fix a number of other problems that are plaguing our schools.

LESSON 13

PRACTICE 1 and 2

Below are two possible conclusions for the school uniforms essay.

Closing with a question:

> Of course, school uniforms won't solve every problem. Poor kids will still be poor, violent students may still be violent, and advertisements will still assail us with the message that you can get what you want (the right guy, the right girl, the right friends, the right job) by buying and wearing trendy clothes. But school uniforms can help equalize the incredible division between the fashion "have's" and the "have not's"; they can improve discipline; and they can improve learning. In the same year that disciplinary incidents went down at Jamestown High, SAT scores went up. Wouldn't you like your school to do the same?

Closing with a call to action.

> School uniforms aren't a cure-all, but in all of the public schools where school uniforms are now required, attendance and test scores are up, and disciplinary incidents are down. Students attest to feeling like they're part of a community, and most say they like not having to worry about what to wear. More importantly, most say they actually feel better about themselves and school than they ever did before.
>
> The power to create this kind of positive change is in your hands. Talk to your PTA and school board representatives. Show them the facts. Start a campaign to make school uniforms part of your child's education. You'll be glad you did—and so will they.

LESSON 14

PRACTICE 1

Answers will vary. Here's an additional supporting paragraph:

> Here's another example. Imagine you're at a diner. When the waitress hands you your check, you notice that she made a mistake, charging you $12.58 instead of $15.58. But you don't tell her. Instead, you pay $12.58 and pocket the $3.00 difference.

PRACTICE 2

Answers will vary. Here's an example of how to revise and expand one of the paragraphs in the "lying with silence" essay:

Original:

> I'm guilty, too. I knew my friend's boyfriend was also seeing someone else. But I kept quiet. I helped to keep her in the dark. Then, when she found him out—and found out I'd known about it—it was terrible. It destroyed their relationship, and our friendship.

Revised and expanded:

I'm guilty of silent deceptions, too. For example, last year, I discovered that my friend Amy's boyfriend, Scott, was seeing someone else on the side. But I kept quiet about it because I didn't want to hurt Amy. A few weeks later, someone else told her about Scott's two-timing—and told her that I knew about it.

Amy couldn't believe that I deceived her like that. She felt just as betrayed as if I'd lied to her face about it. Scott's deception ruined their relationship. My deception destroyed our friendship.

LESSON 15

PRACTICE 1

As usual, answers will vary, but your table should look something like the following:

Paragraph	Idea	Function
3	when silence is a lie	addressing possible counter-argument (that being silent isn't lying)
4	man who lies about HIV	offers example of lie
5	consequences of his lie	offers evidence that silent lie is devastating
6	lying to Amy about Scott and consequences of that lie	offers another example and evidence of consequences
7	lying at diner	offers another example of silent lie
8	silent lies can be devastating; prosecute people who lie about HIV	concludes essay

1. The essay is organized by order of importance, from most to least important.

2. Probably not. For arguments, the best strategy is typically least to most important.

3. Reverse the order of the examples. Start with the diner scenario. Keep the Amy/Scott example second, and then end with the most powerful and convincing example—the man who lied about his HIV status.

PRACTICE 2

Answers will vary. Here's one way to revise the conclusion:

Silence can not only be deceitful—it can also be deadly. Before you decide to deceive someone with silence, consider the consequences of your action, and recognize your action for what it is: a lie.

LESSON 16

PRACTICE 1

Individual revisions will vary, but you should have addressed the following problems in the paragraph:

1st sentence: unnecessary repetition and wordiness
2nd sentence: unnecessary repetition and wordiness as well as passive sentence
3rd sentence: pretentious language and wordiness
4th sentence: passive sentence
5th sentence: unnecessary repetition and possible ambiguity (does "they" refer to questions or opportunities?)

Here's how your revised paragraph might look:

> The greatest challenge my generation will face will be ethical dilemmas created by scientific advances. We have discovered so much in this century, especially in the last few decades. We have opportunities to do things we never thought possible before. But these opportunities have raised some very difficult ethical questions. These opportunities have given us new power over nature, but this power can easily be abused.

PRACTICE 2

Individual revisions will vary. Here's one possibility:

> My generation will face many problems. First is the problem of feeling overwhelmed by technology. Second, with the ever-increasing life span of human beings, the generation gap is widening. A third problem is the population explosion; there are more people on this planet than ever before, and the world population continues to grow exponentially, putting a squeeze on our habitable space. That leads us to a fourth problem: limited natural resources.

LESSON 17

PRACTICE 1

Answers will vary slightly. Here's the paragraph with run-ons, fragments and tense shifts corrected:

> Comic relief is important in tragedies. Readers need a little relief from all of the sadness in the story. For example, let's consider *Hamlet*. After Ophelia dies, the next scene is with the grave digger, who is a very funny character. He digs up a skull and makes a long speech about who the skull might have belonged to. Even though it is about death, the scene is funny, and it allows readers to forget about the tragedy for a moment and laugh.

PRACTICE 2

Answers will vary slightly. Here's the paragraph with capitalization, punctuation, and spelling errors corrected:

> Did you know that before Galileo, most people believed that the Earth was the center of the universe? Galileo discovered many things, including the telescope, the law of falling bodies, and the moons around Jupiter. But Galileo's most important discovery was definitely the true structure of the solar system. He proved that the planets revolve around the sun; instead of everything revolving around the Earth.

LESSON 18

PRACTICE 1

Answers will vary. Here's one possibility:

Thesis: One of today's unsung heroes is my friend Anne Sullivan.

Outline:

1. How I met Anne
   - behind her in line at the store
   - she was buying diapers
   - couldn't believe how many she was buying
   - I asked if she needed help carrying them to her car
   - found out she had just adopted five orphans from Romania

2. Meeting the orphans
   - told Anne I loved children
   - she invited me to come by and help out
   - went the next day
     - saw how great she was with the babies
     - saw how ill most of them looked

3. Why she adopted
   - told me about the orphanages in Romania
     - so overcrowded, babies starved for attention and affection
   - she'd had very loving parents and couldn't have any children of her own
   - family connections made it possible to adopt more than one child

4. How can she handle it?
   - Anne's job—low paying (librarian), but flexible hours and close by
   - close network of family and friends to help out
   - me deciding to help out, too

5. Why is she a hero?

- forever changed the lives of five children
- giving them a chance to grow up in a safe, loving home
- setting an example for others, like me
- a year later, babies all healthy, happy, well adjusted

Conclusion: Now when Anne goes to buy diapers, she always has someone to help—me.

LESSONS 19 & 20

PRACTICE

To estimate a grade for your timed essay, take another look at the scoring chart on pages 170–171. Read your essay and evaluate it by using this special scoring system. After you assign a number for each of the categories shown on the scoring chart, average the numbers to get an overall score. A 5 is an "A," a 4 is a "B," a 3 is a "C," a 2 is a "D," and a 1 is an "F." What grade did your essay get?

POST-TEST
Part I

If you miss any of the answers, you can find help for that kind of question in the lesson shown to the right of the answer.

Question	Answer	Lesson
1	b	1, 2
2	d	1
3	c	12
4	a	9
5	d	6, 7
6	b	10
7	d	9, 15
8	a	2
9	c	14-17
10	b	16
11	a	13
12	a	6, 7
13	c	17
14	b	18
15	b	12
16	d	16

17	e	5, 8

Question	Answer	Lesson
18	b	5, 6
19	d	15
20	a	11

Part II

Use the Scoring Chart on pages 170–171 to evaluate your essay. After you assign a number for each of the categories shown on the scoring chart, average the numbers to get an overall score.

APPENDIX

ere is a list of additional resources you may want to consult for more information about writing essays.

GENERAL ESSAY WRITING

Arlov, Pamela. *Wordsmith: A Guide to Paragraphs and Short Essays.* Prentice Hall, 1999.

Campbell, Martha. *Focus: Writing Paragraphs and Essays.* Prentice Hall, 1998.

Dean, Kitty Chen. *Essentials of the Essay: Writing, Reading, and Grammar.* Allyn & Bacon, 1998.

Donald, Robert B., et. al. *Writing Clear Essays.* Prentice Hall, 1995.

Dorn, David. *Building Essays: A Reader Centered Writing Guide.* NY: Prentice Hall, 1999.

Germov, John. *Get Great Marks for Your Essays.* Allen & Unwin, 1997.

Hairston, Maxine, et. al. *Coretext: A Handbook for Writers.* Addison-Wesley, 1997.

Harris, Jeanette, and Ann Moseley. *Strategies for College Writing: Sentences, Paragraphs, Essays.* Allyn & Bacon, 2000.

McCall, John, and Harry Teitelbaum. *How to Write Themes and Essays.* IDG Worldwide, 1998.

McClain, Molly, and Jacqueline Roth. *Schaum's Quick Guide to Writing Great Essays.* McGraw-Hill, 1998.

Meriwether, Nell. *Strategies for Writing Successful Essays.* NTC Publishing, 1997.

Meyers, Alan. *Composing With Confidence: Writing Effective Paragraphs and Essays.* Addison-Wesley, 1999.

Raimes, Ann. *Keys for Writers: A Brief Handbook.* Houghton Mifflin, 1999.

Scarry, Sandra, and John Scarry. *The Writer's Workplace: Paragraphs to Essays—Building College Writing Skills.* Harcourt Brace Jovanovich, 1996.

Stanford, Gene, and Marie Smith. *Better Writing: From Paragraph to Essay.* Harcourt Brace Jovanovich, 1997.

Trimble, John. *Writing with Style: Conversations on the Art of Writing.* 2nd ed. Prentice Hall, 1999.

Winkler, Anthony, and Jo Ray McCuen. *Writing Talk: Paragraphs and Short Essays.* Prentice Hall, 1997.

STYLE

Bates, Jefferson. *Writing with Precision: How to Write So That You Cannot Possibly Be Misunderstood.* Penguin, 2000.

Campbell, Dianna. *Better Sentence Writing in 30 Minutes a Day.* Career Press, 1995.

Cook, Claire Kehrwald. *Line by Line: How to Improve Your Own Writing.* Houghton Mifflin, 1986.

Glaser, Joe. *Understanding Style: Practical Ways to Improve Your Writing.* Oxford University Press, 1998

Hacker, Diana. *A Pocket Style Manual.* 3rd ed. Bedford/St. Martins, 2000.

Hoffman, Gary, and Glynis Hoffman. *Adios, Strunk and White.* 2nd ed. Verve Press, 1999.

Provost, Gary. *100 Ways to Improve Your Writing.* Mentor Books, 1985.

Richardson, Peter. *Style: A Pragmatic Approach.* Allyn & Bacon, 1998.

Strunk, William, and E. B. White. *The Elements of Style.* 4th ed. Allyn & Bacon, 1999.

Waddell, Marie, et. al. *The Art of Styling Sentences: 20 Patterns for Success.* 3rd ed. Barrons, 1993.

Williams, Joseph. *Style: Ten Lessons in Clarity and Grace.* 6th ed. Addison-Wesley, 1999.

GRAMMAR AND MECHANICS

Adams, Peter. *Basics: A Grammar and Punctuation Workbook.* Addison-Wesley, 1998.

Beason, Larry and Mark Lester. *A Commonsense Guide to Grammar and Usage.* Bedford, 1999.

Devine, Joe. *Commas Are Our Friends.* Green Stone Publications, 1988.

Feierman, JoAnne. *Actiongrammar: Fast, No-Hassle Answers on Everyday Usage and Punctuation.* Fireside, 1995.

Goddin, Nell and Erik Palma. *Grammar Smart: A Guide to Perfect Usage.* Villard Books, 1993.

Hollander, Joseph, ed. *21st Century Grammar Handbook.* Dell, 1993.

Immel, Constance and Florence Sacks. *Better Grammar in 30 Minutes a Day.* Career Press, 1995.

Stilman, Anne. *Grammatically Correct: The Writer's Essential Guide to Punctuation, Spelling, Style, Usage and Grammar.* Writers Digest Books, 1997.

COLLEGE APPLICATION ESSAYS

Bauld, Harry. *On Writing the College Application Essay*. Barnes & Noble, 1987.

Burnham, Amy, et. al. *Essays That Will Get You into College*. Barrons, 1998.

Davidson, Wilma, and Susan McCloskey. *Writing a Winning College Application Essay*. Peterson's Guides, 1996.

Ehrenhaft, George. *Writing a Successful College Application Essay: The Key to College Admission*. Barrons, 1993.

Georges, Christopher, and Gigi Georges. *100 Successful College Application Essays*. Mentor Books, 1991.

Mason, Michael. *How to Write a Winning College Application Essay*. 3rd ed. Prima, 1997.

McGinty, Sarah Myers. *The College Application Essay*. College Entrance Examination Board, 1997.

Nourse, Kenneth A. *How to Write Your College Application Essay*. VGM Career Horizons, 1993.

Power, Hele, and Robert Diantonio. *The Admissions Essay: Clear and Effective Guidelines on How to Write That Most Important College Entrance Essay*. Lyle Stuart, 1998.

Stewart, Mark Alan, and Cynthia Muchnick. *The Best College Admission Essays*. IDG Worldwide, 1997.

Van Raalte, Susan. *College Applications and Essays*. 3rd ed. IDG Worldwide, 1997.

CONTENTS

CONTENTS (continued)

INTRODUCTION

Essays. Some people actually enjoy writing them; others would rather copy over the dictionary by hand than write an essay. If you fall into the first category, congratulations—you've already won half the battle. If you fall into the second category—and if you've bought this book, chances are you do—then take heart. The lessons that follow will give you simple, practical, clear guidelines for writing more effective essays. You still might not *enjoy* writing essays by the time you finish this book, but you will certainly have a better understanding of the writing process, and you'll feel much more confident in your ability to handle many different essay writing situations.

HOW TO USE THIS BOOK

This book is designed to help you improve your essay writing skills in just a few weeks. Each lesson focuses on a specific aspect of the writing process and should take about 20 minutes to complete. If you read one chapter per day, Monday through Friday, and do all of the exercises carefully, you should become a more powerful and effective writer by the end of one month of study.

Although each lesson is designed to be an effective skill builder on its own, it is important that you proceed through this book in order, from Lesson 1 through Lesson 20. If you don't work through the lessons in Section I, you won't get the full benefit of the lessons in Section II. That's because writing is a process: a series of skills, strategies, and approaches that writers use to create effective essays. In reality, this process is not as linear as it is presented in the book. But once you understand the writing process, you can adapt it to your unique working style and to each specific writing situation.

The book is divided into four sections that take you through the different steps in the writing process. The first section, Planning the Essay, covers the basic pre-writing and planning strategies so essential to effective writing. The second section, Drafting the Essay, shows you how to take your ideas and formulate a solid working draft of your essay. The third section, Revising and Editing, shows you how you can take that draft and shape it into an essay that is clear, powerful, and effective. Finally, the fourth section, Taking an Essay Exam, provides strategies for dealing with one of the most difficult writing situations students face: the in-class timed essay exam.

Each lesson provides several exercises that allow you to practice the skills you learn throughout the book. The exercises aren't simply matching or multiple-choice questions. Instead, you'll be putting the skills you learn into immediate practice by doing your own writing. These practice exercises are central to your success with this book. No matter how many examples you see, you really won't benefit from these lessons *unless you try the exercises yourself.* The only way you can improve your writing is with practice. Remember to keep your answers to the practice exercises as you move though the book. Some lessons will ask you to further develop ideas you generated in earlier practice exercises.

To help you stay on track, sample answers and explanations for the practice exercises are provided at the back of the book. Keep in mind that these answers are always *suggested* or *possible* answers. When it comes to real writing, each person's answer will be different. Read the explanations carefully as you review your response to the exercise.

You'll also find practical skill-building ideas at the end of each lesson: simple thinking or writing tasks you can do throughout the day or the week to sharpen the skills you learn in that lesson.

To help you gauge your progress, this book begins with a writing pretest. You should take this pretest *before* you start Lesson 1. Then, after you've finished Lesson 20, take the post-test. The tests are different but comparable, so you will be able to see just how much your understanding of the writing process and your writing and revising skills have improved.

DIFFERENT TYPES OF ESSAYS

What makes writing both so interesting and so challenging is that every writing task is unique. Writing is communication: You are expressing ideas about a *subject* to an *audience* for a *purpose*. And each time you sit down to write, one or more of these three elements will be different, creating a completely unique writing situation.

Essays are one of many different forms, or genres, of writing. And while there are many different kinds of essays one could write, there are some general skills and strategies that apply to all types of essays. This book will teach you those skills and strategies and help you practice them in regard to four specific kinds of essay writing tasks:

- the college application essay

- the SAT II Writing Test essay exam
- the essay component of an Advanced Placement (AP) essay exam
- essays for high school and college classes (both in-class timed essays and out-of-class essays)

This section briefly describes each of these writing situations and offers some general advice on how to best handle these writing tasks. You'll be able to better apply many of the suggestions offered here after you've finished this book, which breaks down the steps in the writing process and provides specific strategies for more effective essays.

THE COLLEGE APPLICATION ESSAY

Most colleges and universities require students to submit a written essay with their application. You may be given a very specific topic to write about, or you may be asked to come up with a topic of your own.

The essay portion of an application is a very important tool for admissions officers. The essay gives admissions officers what test scores and high school grades can't: a sense of who you are and what you're all about. From your essay, admissions officers draw conclusions about:

Your personality. Who are you? What makes you unique?

Your creativity. How do you approach a topic that hundreds of other students also address? How do you express yourself?

How you develop ideas. Are your ideas logical? Do you think things through?

Your vision and goals. What's important to you? What do you want to accomplish?

Your character and values. What kind of choices have you made/would you make? Why?

Your ability to analyze, to make connections, and to draw conclusions. How do you make sense of things? What do you think about the world around you?

A good application essay can transform you from a two-dimensional applicant into a dynamic, three-dimensional, "real" person. And in most cases, the more real you are to admissions officers, the more likely you are to be accepted.

Of course, the application essay also gives readers a sense of how well you are able to communicate in writing. And your ability to communicate in writing is crucial to your academic success. After all, admissions officers are not only looking to see if you're a good fit for the university—they also want to see that you'll be able to handle their curriculum and that you'll be able to read and write effectively on the college level.

Types of Essay Assignments

Most college applications assign one of three types of essays:

1. The "about you" essay.
2. The "about us" essay.
3. The open or creative essay.

A brief description and examples of each type follow. For more details and tips on the college application essay, visit the College Board's Web site at http://www.collegeboard.com/collapps/essay.

The "About You" Essay

This assignment asks you to tell readers about yourself. It usually asks you to describe your personality or a particularly memorable experience—a time you learned something important about yourself or the world around you. Here are a few examples:

"Write an essay which conveys to the reader a sense of who you are." (Columbia University)

"Describe the most challenging obstacle you have had to overcome; discuss its impact, and tell what you have learned from the experience." (Guilford College)

"To learn to think is to learn to question. Discuss a matter you once thought you knew 'for sure,' that you learned to question." (Bryn Mawr College)

The "About Us" Essay

This assignment asks you to explain why you are applying to that particular college or university. Why did you choose that school? What do you like about it? How can that college help you achieve your goals? By asking these questions, admissions officers can find out what your goals are and how serious you are about your education. Here are some sample assignments:

"Describe your reasons for selecting Loyola College and your personal and professional goals and plans for after college." (Loyola College)

"Why is UVM a good college choice for you?" (University of Vermont)

"Please relate your interest in studying at Georgetown University to your future goals." (Georgetown University)

The Open or Creative Essay

These assignments allow you to reveal yourself in more expressive ways because they give you much more freedom in choosing your topic. Indeed, a key consideration for readers of these essays is just what you decide to write about and how you decide to write about it. The amount of freedom and creativity varies. Some applications even allow you to submit a short piece of fiction. Here are some examples of typical open/creative essay assignments:

"In your opinion, what is the greatest challenge your generation will face? What ideas do you have for dealing with this issue?" (College of the Holy Cross)

"You have just completed your 300-page autobiography. Please submit page 217." (University of Pennsylvania)

"Ask and answer the one important question which you wish we had asked." (Carleton College)

Tips for Success

In addition to the writing skills you'll learn throughout this book, there are a few specific strategies that will help you create a successful college application essay:

- Be original. Admissions officers read thousands of essays each year. An essay that is original—one that deals with a unique topic or approaches a standard topic from a unique angle—will help your application stand out from the others.

- Be natural. If you're trying to sound like someone else, your essay will come across sounding false. This creates the impression that you lack self-confidence or self-awareness. It could also be interpreted as a sign that someone else wrote your essay for you. So, be yourself. After all, that's what readers really want to know about.

- Be thoughtful. Spend time thinking about how you will address the assignment. This will help you be both original and natural in your essay. Readers can tell when an essay was dashed off without too much thought. It will lack originality, and it will be disorganized and underdeveloped. Do lots of brainstorming before you begin to write.

- Be correct. Use standard English and proofread carefully. You don't want admissions officers to think you don't really care about your application—but that's just the impression you'll give if you submit a poorly proofread essay. An essay full of errors sends the message that you are either inconsiderate (you don't care about your readers enough to give them clean copy) or that you haven't mastered standard English—and that suggests that you'll have problems in the college classroom.

THE SAT II WRITING TEST

While the SAT I: Reasoning Test attempts to measure your general verbal, mathematics, and reasoning skills, the SAT II: Subject Tests are designed to measure how much you know about a specific discipline. The difference is worth repeating: On the SAT II, it's not how you think, but what you know…mostly. The exception is the SAT II Writing Test, a one-hour exam that includes a 20-minute essay component. The essay exam is designed to gauge the following:

- Your thinking skills. How well can you organize your thoughts in a short period of time?
- Your self-expression. How well can you communicate your ideas in written English?
- Your mastery of standard English. How correctly do you communicate your ideas?

Evaluation

Each SAT II Writing Test is read by two readers, both of whom give the essay a score between 1–6:

    1–2 = Below Average
    3–4 = Average
    5–6 = Above Average

The essays are graded *holistically,* which means they're graded for their cumulative effect—the overall impact they make on the reader. Everything counts: content, style, and grammatical correctness. Essays are graded both on their own and on comparable merit. That is, readers look at how well an essay works individually and how it compares to the other essays in the group. In general, quality is more important than quantity (a rule of thumb for all essays), but of course the essay must be long enough to have sufficiently developed ideas.

Types of Assignments

Unlike the college application essay, the SAT II Writing Test essay doesn't offer much choice in your assignment. You are given one topic and you must respond to that topic in the way the test describes. Like college application essays, the SAT II Writing Test essay assignments fall into three categories.

Fill in the Blank

Fill in the blank assignments ask you to complete a statement and explain why you completed it that way. Here's an example:

> *"I've done many things in my life that I'm proud of, but one thing that I'm especially proud of is _____." Write an essay that completes the statement above. Explain the reasons behind your choice.*

Responding to a Quotation

Responding to a quotation assignments give you a quotation and ask you to respond to that quotation. Usually, you will be asked to agree or disagree and explain why. Here's an example:

> *"Problems are opportunities in disguise." Write an essay in which you agree or disagree with this statement. Use your personal experience, current events, or history, literature, or any other discipline to support your answer.*

Responding to a Statement, Issue, or Situation

Responding to a statement, issue, or situation assignments usually present a controversial issue or complex situation and ask you to take and defend a position. Here's an example:

> *Some people believe that there is such a thing as a just war. Are there any circumstances in which war is justified? Please use specific examples to explain your answer.*

For more information on the SAT II Writing Test, visit the College Board's SAT II Web site at http://www.collegeboard.org/SAT.

Tips for Success

Here are a few strategies for a successful SAT II Writing Test essay:

- Respond to the assignment. As uninspiring as an essay assignment may seem to you, it has been chosen because it is something to which all test takers should be able to develop an interesting response. (We all have experiences that we're proud of, we all have opinions about war, and so on). Further, because the tests are graded holistically and comparatively, evaluators need some sort of consistency among essays—otherwise it becomes difficult to gauge things like the originality of your thesis or the strength of your support. The directions on the SAT II Writing Test specifically state that you must write on the assigned topic. You will automatically lose points if you don't respond to the assignment.

- Be creative. Everyone will be responding to the same assignment. If your essay stands out because it is original, readers will view your essay more positively. Think carefully about how you can approach the topic in an interesting way.

- Remember the purpose of the test. Remember that your main goal isn't to show readers who you are but rather *how you write*. It's not so much the story you tell (though it should be interesting), but *how well you tell it*. You need to craft a clear and correct essay that provides sufficient support for your ideas. Most questions ask for your opinion, and a strong essay will support your opinions with specific examples and evidence.

THE ADVANCED PLACEMENT ESSAY EXAM

Advanced Placement (AP) courses give high school students the opportunity to earn college-level credit for their course work. Each May, students in AP courses can take AP exams to demonstrate that they have mastered the course material. There are 31 different AP exams in 16 different disciplines. All AP exams except Studio Art now include both multiple choice and free response essay questions. Colleges review student AP exam scores and determine whether or not students should be granted credit for equivalent college-level courses.

Evaluation

AP exams receive a score from 1–5, where a 1 means no recommendation for credit and a 5 means the student is extremely qualified to earn credit. Most colleges and universities will consider a score of 3, but credit is usually granted only for scores of 4 or 5, depending upon the match between the AP course and the college's curriculum.

While AP essay exams are evaluated much like the SAT II Writing Tests, readers are looking for a very different kind of essay. SAT II Writing Test readers are primarily concerned with how well you can express and support your ideas. On AP essays, however, readers are looking for:

how well you understand the subject matter
how clearly you explain concepts
how well you apply strategies and approaches of the discipline

In general, AP essays, like SAT II Writing Tests, are graded holistically, but because of the emphasis on subject matter, the *content* of your essay carries a bit more weight than style and correctness. An essay that thoroughly, clearly, and accurately answers the question (demonstrating that you thoroughly understand the material) would still receive a high score even if it lacked stylistic flair and contained a few grammatical mistakes. If that same essay were loaded with grammar mistakes, however, the score would be considerably lower. Likewise, an essay that is beautifully written but fails to demonstrate understanding of the material will receive a lower score.

Three Examples

The English Literature AP Exam

In addition to multiple choice questions (worth 45 percent of the exam), the English Literature AP Exam includes three essays which count for the remaining 55 percent. Students are allowed 40 minutes for each essay. In the three essays, students are asked to do the following:

1. Analyze a specific poem.
2. Analyze a specific prose passage (a short story, excerpt from a novel, or essay).
3. Use their own readings to respond to a literary topic.

Here's an example of the first kind of essay assignment:

Read the following poem carefully. Write a well-organized essay in which you discuss the poem, noting in particular the author's use of language, structure, and imagery.

FOG
The fog comes
on little cat feet.

It sits looking
over harbor and city
on silent haunches
and then moves on.
　　　　—Carl Sandburg (1916)

The second essay assignment is similar to the first; it asks you to analyze a selected prose passage. But for the third essay, you decide which texts to discuss. Here's an example:

Write an essay in which you discuss how comic relief works in a tragedy. Use one or more stories, novels, or plays to illustrate your ideas.

The Biology AP Exam

The Biology AP Exam includes four essays that must be completed in 90 minutes. Students are encouraged to include figures and graphs wherever possible. Students will have to write one essay about molecules and cells, one about heredity and evolution, and two about organisms and populations. Here's a sample essay assignment:

> *Describe the process of photosynthesis. What are the major plant pigments involved in photosynthesis? Design an experiment to measure the rate of photosynthesis.*

The U.S. History AP Exam

This exam gives students 130 minutes to write three essays. First, students are given 15 minutes to read 6–12 documents. Then, for the first essay, students must analyze the documents in relation to a particular historical circumstance, event, issue, or theme. For the second essay, students can choose one of two questions about U.S. history from Colonization to Reconstruction. For the third essay, students choose one of two questions about U.S. history from Reconstruction to the present.

Here's a sample essay question about recent U.S. history:

> *What were the issues, successes, and failures of the Civil Rights movement from the 1960s through the 1970s?*

Tips for Success

Here are some strategies for a successful AP exam essay:

- Know the material. Remember, this essay is not about who you are, but what you know about the subject.
- Respond to the assignment. Readers are looking for evidence that you have mastered *specific* material. You need to fulfill the assignment and show that you know that material.
- Be specific. Provide details and examples whenever possible. This shows that you have a thorough understanding of the material and that you are able to apply specific concepts from the discipline.
- Be clear and correct. While grammatical correctness isn't the main thing evaluators are looking for, it *is* important that readers be able to understand your ideas.

ESSAYS FOR HIGH SCHOOL AND COLLEGE CLASSES

In just about any high school or college class, you can expect at least part, if not all, of your evaluation for the term to be based upon your written work. In a college literature class, for example, 100 percent of your grade might be based on two out-of-class essays, an in-class midterm, and final essay exams. In a political science class, your midterm and final exams might include multiple-choice, short answer, and essay questions. So your success in school depends heavily upon your ability to write effectively, both in and out of the classroom.

Types of Essay Assignments

Essay assignments in high school and college classes will be as varied as the instructors who teach them. Most assignments, however, will fall into one of two categories:

The Personal Essay

In composition classes and in college placement exams, you will often be asked to write an essay based on your personal experience and observation. These essay assignments might look much like an SAT II Writing Test assignment. Here are two examples:

Alison Lurie wrote, "Long before I am near enough to talk to you in the street or at a party, you announce your personality and opinions to me through what you are wearing. By the time we meet and converse, we have already spoken to each other in an older and more universal language: the language of clothing." Write an essay in which you agree or disagree with this statement. Use evidence from your personal experience, observations, or reading to support your position.

Describe a time when you presented yourself as believing in something you really did not believe in. Why did you present yourself that way? What were the consequences, if any of this misrepresentation? How would you present yourself in a similar situation today? Explain.

The Analysis Essay

In most other classes, essay assignments will often ask you to *analyze* specific texts, ideas, or issues. Here are several examples from different disciplines.

From a religious point of view, what is truth? Use examples from two different religions to support your answer.

Analyze a local television news program. What stories and events get coverage? How are these stories and events covered? What values and beliefs about America, about the world, about television and its viewers do you think the news program's coverage reflects?

What illusions does Renoir's film La Grande Illusion *refer to? Discuss those illusions and how the historical events that led to World War I helped to foster them.*

Compare and contrast the principles and applications of the following types of therapies:

- *psychotherapy*
- *group therapy*
- *drug therapy*

Be sure to include an account of the origin and development of each therapy.

Tips for Success

Here are some strategies for successful high school and college out-of-class essays:

- Fulfill the assignment. Have a clear thesis that directly responds to the assignment.

- Provide solid support. Whether you're writing a personal essay or an analysis essay, you need to show readers that your thesis is valid. Support your ideas with specific evidence and examples.

- Be correct. You need to convey your ideas clearly to your reader. Make sure your sentences are clear and free of errors.

- Write with style. Most of your essays will be on the formal side, but that doesn't mean they have to be dull and dry. Use vivid verbs, specific nouns, and an occasional striking simile or metaphor.

Here are some strategies for successful high school and college in-class timed essays:

- Create an outline. As soon as you determine your thesis, draft an outline to organize your ideas. Be as specific as possible.

- Don't get hung up on the introduction. As long as you have your thesis, you can jump right in. Get moving. Save space at the top of the page to fill in the introduction later.

- Save time to revise. You're under pressure, and that means you're more likely to make mistakes. Give your essay at least a quick "once-over" to make sure you didn't miss any words or make silly time-pressure mistakes, like writing "Ronald McDonald" when you really mean "Ronald Reagan."

PRETEST

Before you begin this book, you may want to get an idea of how much you already know and how much you need to learn about essays and the writing process. If so, take the following pretest.

The pretest consists of two parts. Part I contains 20 multiple-choice questions addressing several of the key concepts in this book. Part II asks you to write your own essay and evaluate it according to the criteria provided.

Even if you get all of the questions on the pretest right and score a 5 on your essay, you will undoubtedly profit from working through the lessons in this book, as only a fraction of the information in the lessons is covered on the pretest. On the other hand, if you miss a lot of questions on the pretest, don't despair. These lessons are designed to teach you essay writing skills step by step. You may find that the lessons take you a little longer than 20 minutes to complete, but that's okay. Take your time and enjoy the learning process.

You can use the space on the pages following Part II of the pretest to record your answers and write your essay. Or, if you prefer, simply circle the answers directly for Part I. If this book doesn't belong to you, don't write in the book. Write the numbers 1–20 on a piece of paper and record your answers there. Use a sheet of loose-leaf or other $8\frac{1}{2} \times 11$ ruled paper for your essay.

You can take as much time as you need for Part I, though it probably shouldn't take you more than 20 minutes. When you've finished, check your answers against the answer key at the end of the book. Each answer tells you which lesson of the book deals with the concept addressed in that question. Set aside another 30 minutes to complete Part II.

PART I

1. All essays should be about five or six paragraphs long.
   a. true
   b. false

2. The best place in an essay for a thesis statement is generally:
   a. the first sentence in an essay
   b. the last sentence in an essay
   c. the end of the introduction
   d. the third paragraph

3. A good introduction should do which of the following?
   a. grab the reader's attention
   b. state the thesis
   c. provide the main supporting ideas for the thesis
   d. (a) and (b)
   e. all of the above

4. Your relationship to your readers has an effect on how you write your essay.
   a. true
   b. false

5. Which of the following best describes the problem with the paragraph below?

   Sullivan studied 25 city playgrounds. He found several serious problems. The playgrounds were dirty. They were also overcrowded. They were also dangerous. Many parks had broken glass everywhere. Many parks also had broken equipment.

   a. lack of variety in sentence structure
   b. grammatical errors
   c. lack of transitions
   d. poor word choice

6. Which organizational strategy does the paragraph above use?
   a. comparison and contrast
   b. chronology
   c. problem-solution
   d. order of importance

7. Read the following essay assignment carefully. Which of the sentences below best describes the kind of essay that you should write?

Some say "ignorance is bliss." Others claim that ignorance is a form of slavery and that only knowledge can set you free. Which view do you think is more accurate? Explain your answer.

a. explain the difference between "ignorance" and "knowledge"
b. explain which belief you agree with and why
c. explain how you think we can improve education
d. discuss the evils of slavery

8. Which of the following organizational patterns applies to *all* essays?

a. order of importance
b. cause and effect
c. assertion → support
d. problem → solution

9. A *thesis* is best defined as:

a. the subject of an essay
b. the main idea of an essay
c. a long essay
d. the way a writer introduces an essay

10. In the paragraph below, the first sentence is best described as which of the following?

More and more Americans are turning to alternative medicine. The ancient art of aromatherapy has gained a tremendous following, particularly on the West coast. Acupuncture, the traditional Chinese art of "needle therapy," has doubled its number of active practitioners. And holistic medicine—treating the whole body instead of just one part—is so popular that some HMOs now even pay for holistic care.

a. a transitional sentence
b. a topic sentence
c. a supporting idea
d. a thesis

11. In the paragraph above, the second sentence is best described as which of the following?

a. a transitional sentence
b. a topic sentence
c. a supporting idea
d. a thesis

12. Which of the following should a conclusion *not* do?

   a. bring in a new idea

   b. restate the thesis in other words

   c. provide a sense of closure

   d. arouse the reader's emotions

13. Words and phrases like "meanwhile," "on the other hand," and "for example" are examples of:

   a. passive words

   b. assertions

   c. modifiers

   d. transitions

14. Which of the following strategies is particularly useful during an essay exam?

   a. brainstorming

   b. freewriting

   c. outlining

   d. glossing

15. Brainstorming typically takes place during which step in the writing process?

   a. planning

   b. drafting

   c. revising

   d. editing

16. "Editing" and "revising" mean essentially the same thing.

   a. true

   b. false

17. Support for a thesis can come in which of the following forms?

   a. specific examples

   b. expert opinion

   c. anecdotes

   d. (a) and (b)

   e. (a), (b) and (c)

18. Never use a one-sentence paragraph.

   a. true

   b. false

19. What is the main problem with the following sentence?

Newman lost the election because of the fact that the opponent whom he ran against had a lot more money for ads.

    a. It's a run-on sentence.
    b. It's not properly punctuated.
    c. It's unnecessarily wordy.
    d. It lacks parallel sentence structure.

20. Which of the following strategies will make an essay more convincing?
    a. avoiding run-on sentences
    b. acknowledging counter-arguments
    c. providing specific examples and details
    d. (b) and (c)
    e. (a) and (c)

PART II

Set a timer for 30 minutes. When you're ready to begin, read the essay assignment below carefully. Use the space below and on the following pages to write your essay. STOP writing when 30 minutes have passed, even if you haven't completed your essay. When you've finished, look at the scoring chart in the answer key to estimate your essay's grade.

ESSAY ASSIGNMENT
Many people have been profoundly affected by great works of art. Describe a work of art—a book, a movie, a photograph, a drawing or painting, a song or musical composition—that had a powerful impact on your life. What work of art was it? How did it affect you? Why?

_____

_____

_____

_____

_____

_____

_____

_____

_____

_____

_____

_____

_____

_____

_____

_____

_____

_____

_____

S·E·C·T·I·O·N 1

PLANNING THE ESSAY

Experienced runners know that it's very important to warm up their muscles before they run. Stretching takes time, but it is time well spent. A good warm-up helps runners improve their performance and enjoy the experience. It also helps prevent injuries.

A good warm-up is also very important for writers. Taking the time to plan your essay can dramatically improve the effectiveness of your writing. The planning strategies that you'll learn in this section will also help eliminate many of the frustrations writers face and make writing a much more enjoyable experience.

L · E · S · S · O · N
THINKING ABOUT AUDIENCE AND PURPOSE

LESSON SUMMARY

The first step toward effective writing is to know whom you're writing for, and why. This lesson explains how to understand your audience and purpose and how these two factors affect your writing.

Imagine you've just had an amazing experience: You were able to save someone's life by performing CPR. You want to describe this experience to three different people: your mother, your closest friend, and the admissions counselor at your first-choice college. Are you going to describe your experience the same way to each of these three people? Of course not. Though your subject might be the same, in each situation, you have a different audience and a different purpose.

Because your audience and purpose are always unique, every communication is different and requires a unique approach to be most effective. Whatever your subject, what you write depends upon whom you're writing for and why you're writing. Therefore, the first rule of thumb for writers is this: Audience and purpose determine what you say—and how you say it.

UNDERSTANDING YOUR AUDIENCE

Now imagine that you've been asked to speak about your life-saving experience at the local YMCA. You expect that your audience will be a mix of adults and children—a small segment of the general public. So you prepare your notes and rehearse your speech. But when you arrive, you see that your audience consists solely of second graders from the local elementary school. Can you go ahead as planned? Probably not—not if you want to keep their attention, and not if you want them to understand your main point.

Understanding your audience is crucial to effective writing (and speaking). To understand your audience, there are a few key questions you should ask before you begin a writing task:

1. Who will read your essay?

2. Why will they read your essay?

3. What do they know about your subject?

4. What is your relationship to the reader?

PINPOINTING YOUR AUDIENCE

The first question to ask is who will read what you're writing. All written communications have an audience—that's why they're written down in the first place. But who?

The General Reader

There is, of course, a real person who will be reading your essay—a teacher, an admissions counselor, an AP test evaluator. And it's important to keep this person in mind as you go through the writing process. In most cases, however, this actual reader is not the person you should be writing for. Unless your assignment specifies otherwise, you should write for a "general audience." You can think of this audience as a friendly group of your peers (but not necessarily your classmates), people who have a wide range of backgrounds and interests, and people who may have some things in common with you but certainly don't know you too well (if at all).

Your actual readers—that is, your instructors, admissions counselors, and exam evaluators—want you to write for a general audience for several reasons. For one thing, it helps to establish a friendly but formal tone. But more importantly, it forces you to frame what you're writing in the appropriate context. For example, in your English Literature class, your actual reader—your teacher—knows the novel you're analyzing inside and out. If you write for her instead of for a general audience, you won't need to explain much about the novel's plot and characters. But your instructor wants to see that you understand the novel and how it develops. She needs to see you explain its ideas in terms of the context of the whole novel.

A Specified Audience

Sometimes your assignment will call for you to write for a specific audience rather than a general reader. You might be asked to do something like the following:

A Martian has just landed in your back yard. He asks where he's landed. You answer, "America." He asks, "What kind of place is America?" Write out your answer in a 2–3 page essay.

For this assignment, you have a very specific audience—and this audience will determine how you address the topic. Once you determine whether you have a general or specific audience, you can determine your audiences' purpose and relationship to the subject.

DETERMINING YOUR AUDIENCE'S PURPOSE

Once you've established *who* will read your essay, it's time to determine *why*. What are they hoping to gain? Specific reasons will vary, of course, but you can make some generalizations. First, you can assume your general audience is reading either to be informed or entertained for the same reasons you might read an article in a magazine or the newspaper. Your actual readers, however, have very specific reasons for reading your essay, which might be generalized as follows:

Who They Are	What They're Looking For
Admissions officers reading college application essays	An engaging essay that reveals your personality, goals, and values; evidence that you can organize your thoughts and communicate clearly.
SAT II Writing Test evaluators	An interesting and coherent essay that shows you can formulate and defend an intelligent opinion on a subject; evidence that you can organize your thoughts logically and write clearly and effectively.
AP Essay Exam evaluators	A clear and cohesive essay that demonstrates mastery of subject matter.
High school and college teachers reading in- and out-of-class essay assignments	A combination of the above: mastery of the material (do you understand the book, concept, issue?); a clear and original thesis; mastery of the essay form (clear thesis, strong support, logical organization); mastery of standard English (clear sentences, few errors).

Here's an example. Imagine that you have been asked to write about a poem. Clearly, you could not write the same essay for a college application and an English Literature AP Exam. You have two different sets of actual readers who want two very different things from you.

Admissions officers, for example, would prefer a very personal response to the poem, one that reveals something about who you are and what is important to you. They might want to know if the poem helps you better understand something about yourself and your values. They might want to know how you understand the poem. What does it mean to you? How does it make you feel? What do you get out of it? How can you relate it to your life?

Readers of the AP English Literature Exam, however, will be looking for something very different. They want to see how well you understand the conventions of poetry and use the elements of poetry to make sense of the poem. They want to see what you believe is the theme of the poem, and why. How does the poem convey this idea? They will expect to see terms like *stanza, alliteration,* and *metaphor* used properly to show that you know the genre well.

THE AUDIENCE'S RELATIONSHIP TO THE SUBJECT

In addition, it's essential to consider the relationship of your audience to your subject. What are they likely to know about your topic? How interested will they be in what you have to say? How likely are they to agree or disagree with your ideas?

What Your Readers Know about the Subject

One of the biggest mistakes writers make is to assume that their readers know what they're talking about. Just because you know your subject intimately doesn't mean your readers do. You need to carefully consider how much your readers may know about your subject. For example, say you've decided to write about your interest in robotics for your college application essay. If you use terms like "range weighted Hough Transform" and "sensor fusion algorithm", chances are your readers won't know what you're talking about. You'll either have to explain your terms or replace the technical jargon with words the average reader can understand.

Similarly, say you decide to write about a novel you love. Can you assume your readers have read the novel? Even if they have, can you assume that they read it recently enough to remember its characters, its plot, its ideas? Unless you know for sure, or unless your assignment so specifies ("assume your readers have read *The Great Gatsby* carefully"), you must provide sufficient background information for your readers. You'll need to briefly summarize the plot and provide context for the specific scenes and issues you'd like to discuss. This is always the case when you're writing for a general audience.

How Your Readers Feel about the Subject

Another important consideration is how your readers might feel about the subject. Are they likely to be interested in it? If not, what can you do to arouse their interest? If you've taken a position on an issue, how likely is it that your readers will share your opinion? If they're likely to disagree, how can you help them to accept—or at least understand—your position? (You'll learn about this issue in Lesson 12.)

YOUR RELATIONSHIP TO READERS

Finally, there's one more key question to ask about your audience: What is your relationship to your readers? This relationship helps determine the style, tone, and format of your essay.

Though the four writing situations discussed in this book are different, your relationship to the actual reader is quite similar in each case: that of evaluatee to evaluator. Your actual readers—college admission officers, SAT II Writing Test readers, AP essay exam readers, and teachers—are reading your essay to evaluate it. That's not to say that they won't also enjoy themselves while they read it (you hope that they do). But they're not picking up your essay primarily for their reading pleasure.

So how does this relationship affect your writing? As an evaluatee, in general, it is in your best interest to be formal (but not stuffy), respectful (but not ingratiating), and courteous (but not sticky sweet). It is also in your best interest to follow all of the guidelines that have been provided for you. For example, if your instructor wants your essay typed, with a 12-point font, double spaced, with one-inch margins, and one staple in the top left-hand corner, that's exactly what you should give her.

PRACTICE 1

1. Briefly explain the difference between "actual reader" and "general reader."

_____

_____

_____

2. Take another look at the Martian in the backyard essay assignment. Then, answer the questions that follow.

A Martian has just landed in your back yard. He (or she) asks where he's landed. You answer, "America." He asks, "What kind of place is America?" Write out your answer in a 2–3 page essay.

a. Who is your audience?

_____

b. Given your audience, how should you approach your topic, and why?

_____

_____

_____

KNOWING YOUR PURPOSE

Whether you're writing a college application essay or an essay for your political science class, one of your goals is to receive a positive evaluation for your essay. But for that to happen, the essay itself must also have a clear purpose.

As important as knowing whom you're writing for is knowing *why* you're writing. What is the goal of your essay? What are you hoping to convey through your writing? If your essay effectively achieves its purpose, you're more likely to achieve your goals of a positive evaluation of it.

In many cases, writers are not clear about their purpose until they've done some writing on the topic. You may find that you need to do some brainstorming or even some drafting before you're clear about your purpose. You may also find that your purpose changes as you write—and that's okay, too. The point is this: The more clearly you can articulate your purpose in the planning stage, the more effective your drafting and revising stages will be.

To help you clarify your purpose, you can try a simple fill-in-the-blank exercise like the following:

My goal in this essay is _____.

Try to find a verb that best describes what you hope your essay will do. You might use more than one verb. Here are some examples.

My goal in this essay is to:

- **demonstrate** that I am a resourceful person
- **explain** why I took a year off after high school and **show** how that year prepared me for college
- **prove** that Victor Frankenstein is more of a monster than his creature

Here are some verbs you might find helpful for describing your purpose:

show	describe	explain	prove	convince
demonstrate	compare	contrast	review	inform
summarize	propose	defend	explore	encourage

By clarifying your audience and purpose, you can help ensure that your essay does what it's supposed to do and that its content, structure, and style will be right for its audience. By taking this prewriting step, you're likely to cut down considerably on revising time later. You'll also write something that effectively achieves its purpose. Knowing what you want to say, to whom, and why is the first step in writing effectively.

PRACTICE 2

For the assignments below, how would you describe your purpose?

Assignment 1

Herman Melville wrote, "He who never made a mistake never made a discovery." In an essay, describe how a mistake you made led to an important discovery.

Example: My goal is to *show* how my mistake taught me an important lesson: If you don't follow directions, someone can get hurt.

1._____

_____

Assignment 2:

Read Langston Hughes' essay "Salvation." In an essay, discuss the central conflict that Hughes' describes. How does Hughes resolve that conflict?

2._____

_____

IN SHORT

Effective writing begins with a clear understanding of audience and purpose. Know your audience: who will read your essay, why they will read it, and what they know about your subject. Consider your relationship to your readers, and be sure to carefully consider your purpose. Why are you writing? What do you hope to achieve in your essay?

Skill Building Until Next Time

Because a clear sense of audience and purpose is so essential to good writing, you should be able to determine the intended audience and purpose of a given text. Take a text—a newsletter, an essay, an article—and read it carefully. Can you tell who the primary audience is? Can you determine what the writer was trying to achieve?

L·E·S·S·O·N

UNDERSTANDING AN ASSIGNED TOPIC

LESSON SUMMARY

This lesson explains how to break down an assignment and understand exactly what is required.

Whether you like the freedom of choosing your own topic or prefer to have the topic chosen for you, one thing is for sure: If you are writing an essay for a college application, the SAT II, an AP exam or a high school or college course, you must fulfill the assignment. If the assignment asks you to write about a particular issue—year-round school, for example—you can't expect to succeed if you write about the need for campaign finance reform. No matter how beautiful your essay may be, you haven't fulfilled a basic obligation to your primary reader. You haven't fulfilled the assignment.

In reality, even the most open-ended essay assignments have some sort of guidelines for you to follow. There may be a certain issue you must address, a certain approach you must take, or a certain length requirement you must meet. And when the topic *isn't* open, you have even more constraints. But that's not necessarily a bad thing. Assignments give you a framework or structure within which to work—and that can help guide you through the writing process. And it can limit the amount of time you'd otherwise spend trying to decide what to write about.

FULFILLING THE ASSIGNMENT

The folks who develop essay assignments for college applications, AP exams, and the SAT put a lot of time and effort into developing their assignments. And you can be sure your high school and college teachers do, too. Assignments are formulated with specific goals in mind. Test developers and instructors want to bring out a certain quality in you—your personality, your knowledge, whatever it is they need to see in order to properly understand and evaluate you.

You may think that writing about something other than what's assigned portrays you as an independent thinker, someone who can come up with ideas and doesn't need to be told what to do. But that's not the message you send if you don't fulfill the assignment. By doing your own thing, you tell readers that you either don't care what they want, or you don't know enough about the assigned material to write about it.

Fulfilling the assignment, on the other hand, sends a positive message to readers. It tells them that:

1. You know how to follow directions.

2. You can handle the subject matter.

3. You can meet the challenge they've presented for you.

Additionally, in timed writing situations, fulfilling the assignment shows that:

4. You can organize your thoughts about a specific topic while under pressure.

UNDERSTANDING THE ASSIGNMENT

In order to fulfill the assignment, you must understand exactly what the assignment asks you to do. This is not necessarily as easy as it sounds, because essay assignments aren't always crystal clear. What does it mean, for example, to "discuss" an experience? How are you supposed to "analyze" an issue?

BREAKING DOWN THE ASSIGNMENT

To understand an assignment, you need to make sure you understand both of the following:

(a)   what you are to respond to (the topic)
(b)   how you are to respond to it

In some cases, there may be more than one topic and more than one way you are supposed to respond. To find out exactly what you're expected to do, break down the assignment. First underline the words that describe the topic. Then, circle all of the words that tell you how to respond to the topic. These "direction words" include words like *analyze, describe, discuss, explain, evaluate, identify, illustrate* and *argue (you'll find a more complete list on page 16).*

For example, look at how many parts and direction words there are in the following sample assignment from the AP Biology Exam. First, here is the assignment as it would appear on the exam:

Describe the chemical nature of genes. Discuss the replicative process of DNA in eukaryotic organisms. Be sure to include the various types of gene mutations that can occur during replication.

If you break down the assignment, you can see it actually has three different subjects and three different direction words. The subjects are underlined and the direction words are circled below:

(Describe) *the* chemical nature of genes. (Discuss) *the* replicative process of DNA in eukaryotic organisms. *Be sure to* (include) *the* various types of gene mutations that can occur during replication.

To help make the assignment even more manageable, break down the two parts (the topic and the direction words) into a simple chart:

Subject	Directions
1. The chemical nature of genes	Describe
2. The replicative process of DNA in eukaryotic organisms	Discuss
3. The various types of gene mutations that can occur during replication	Include

To completely fulfill the assignment, you must cover all three of these subjects in the manner in which the assignment describes.

When the Assignment Is a Question

In some assignments, you are given questions instead of direction words. Here's an example:

What were the issues, successes, and failures of the Civil Rights movement from the 1960s through the 1970s?

The subjects are clear, but how exactly are you supposed to deal with them? Where are the direction words?

When you're faced with this kind of assignment, you'll have to use your sense of logic to determine the right direction word. Look carefully at the question. Notice it begins with "What were." This is a good clue that you should *identify* the issues, successes, and failures.

Translating questions into directions can be tricky, but it's important to try to determine exactly how you're supposed to respond to the subject. The following chart lists common question words and the direction words that usually correspond.

Question words	What they usually mean
What is/are…	Define or identify
What caused…	Identify or explain
How are/does…	Explain or evaluate
How is X like…	Compare
How is X different…	Contrast
In what way…	Illustrate
Do you agree?	Argue
Why is/does…	Explain
What do you think of X?	Evaluate

PRACTICE 1

Read the essay topics below carefully. Use the Subject and Directions columns in the tables provided to break them down into their parts. (NOTE: You may not fill each table.)

1. *Describe the change in citizens' attitude towards the presidency in the last decade. Explain what you believe to be the causes of this change. Finally, assess the impact of this attitude on the power of the president.*

Subject	Directions

2. *In Edith Wharton's novella* Summer, *does Charity Royall have control over her destiny? Explain your answer.*

Subject   Directions
_____

_____

_____

_____

_____

_____

3. *Describe in detail the Paracelsian cosmos. How is it similar to the Aristotelian cosmos? How is it different? How is Paracelsus' notion of disease connected with his cosmology? How is it different from Galen's notion of disease?*

Subject   Directions
_____

_____

_____

_____

_____

_____

UNDERSTANDING DIRECTION WORDS

Now that you've broken down the assignment, you know *what* you're supposed to do. But, *how* do you do it? What do these direction words really mean?

To help you make more sense of your essay assignments, take a look at the table below. You'll find the most common essay direction words and their explanations.

Term	Meaning
Analyze	Divide the issue into its main parts and discuss each part. Consider how the parts interact and how they work together to form the whole.
Argue	Express your opinion about the subject and support it.
Assess	See evaluate.
Classify	Organize the subject into groups and explain why this grouping makes sense.
Compare	Point out similarities.
Contrast	Point out differences.

Define	Give the meaning of the subject.
Describe	Show readers what the subject is like; give an account of the subject.
Discuss	Point out the main issues or characteristics of the subject and elaborate.
Evaluate	Make a judgment as to the effectiveness and success of the subject. What is good and bad about it? Why? Describe your criteria for judgment.
Explain	Make your position, an issue, a process, and so on, clear by analyzing, defining, comparing/contrasting, or illustrating.
Identify	Name and describe.
Illustrate	Provide examples of the subject.
Indicate	Explain what you think the subject means and how you came to that interpretation (what makes you think it means X?)
Relate	Point out and discuss connections.
Summarize	Describe the main ideas or points.

For example, look at the following essay assignment:

Compare and contrast Prohibition with the current anti-tobacco movement.

This assignment gives you two direction words: compare and contrast. Thus, you are expected to point out the similarities and differences between the two subjects, Prohibition and the current anti-tobacco movement. Here's another assignment:

Rousseau offers judgments about the relative goodness and badness of life as a savage and of life in society. Assess the validity of these judgments. What arguments does he provide to support them? Are they sound arguments?

The explicit direction word in this assignment is *assess*. The implied direction word for the first question, "What arguments does he provide to support them?" is *identify*. The implied direction word for the second question, "Are they sound arguments?" is *evaluate*. Thus, for this assignment, you will be expected to:

1. Judge the validity and soundness of Rousseau's judgments.

2. Identify the arguments he uses to support his judgments.

PRACTICE 2

Reread the essay topics from Practice 1. Given the direction words, briefly summarize what you think you should be doing in the essay. Do not use the specific direction words in your answers.

1. _____

_____

_____

2. _____

_____

_____

3. _____

_____

_____

IN SHORT

Whatever the writing situation, it's important that you fulfill the requirements of the assignment. To be sure you fulfill your evaluator's expectations, break the assignment down into its parts. Identify the subjects you need to cover and the direction words that tell you how you should address those subjects.

Skill Building Until Next Time

You may not have a reference chart available when you sit down to write an essay. To help familiarize yourself with what each direction word means, write your own assignments using each of the direction words.

BRAINSTORMING TECHNIQUES: FREEWRITING & LISTING

3

LESSON SUMMARY

Even the most experienced writers sometimes have trouble coming up with ideas. This lesson will teach you two important techniques for generating ideas: freewriting and listing.

One of the main reasons students put off essay assignments is because they don't know what to write about. They've been given the freedom to choose their own topic. But instead of feeling liberated, they find themselves wishing someone would just tell them what to write about so they could finally get their paper started.

Even students who normally have no trouble choosing their own topics for out-of-class essays may find themselves in a panic when they have to choose a topic for an in-class essay exam. When you have just 20 or 30 minutes to write, there's no time to waste—so you must be able to pick a good topic, and fast.

Fortunately, there are a few simple strategies you can use for any essay assignment when you have to come up with a topic on your own. These are strategies you can use any time you need to generate ideas.

BRAINSTORMING IDEAS

How do you go about generating ideas for an essay? Maybe if you stare at the blank page long enough, something will come to you. But maybe not. And if you're taking an essay exam, you don't have time to waste. In any case, there are more productive ways to spend your time than being stuck with writer's block.

Different people have different techniques for stimulating their creativity. Some folks like to go for a run or listen to a certain kind of music. You might have something that works for you, and it makes good sense to stick with what you know works. Still, it's worth exploring new strategies. That's why you'll learn four different brainstorming techniques in this and the next lesson:

- freewriting
- listing
- asking questions
- mapping

These brainstorming techniques are tried and true methods for generating ideas. They only take a few minutes, and they can yield wonderful results. If you approach a brainstorming session with an open mind, you'll find yourself coming up with ideas you didn't even realize you had.

Some of these brainstorming techniques are more structured than others, and you might find that one or two work better for you than the rest. But it's important to know how each technique works so that you have several strategies at hand to jump-start your ideas in any writing situation.

FREEWRITING

The freewriting technique is exactly that—*free* writing. There are no constraints. You simply review the assignment and start to write. The only rule is that there are no rules. There is nothing you need to say, and nothing you can't say.

Freewriting allows you to find gems of thought that you might not uncover with a structured approach to the topic. If you let your writing flow freely, some of what you write will be mumbo-jumbo, and some of it might have nothing at all to do with your topic. But if you follow your thoughts where they lead you, you'll find that you have more ideas—and more interesting ideas—about the subject than you realized.

Here are some tips to help your freewriting be more productive:

1. Set a time limit. Limit your freewriting to five or ten minutes at a time. This will force you to get, and keep, moving. It will also help you to write more productively in that time period, since you know you only have a limited amount of time to write.

2. Don't stop writing. Write as much as you can, as fast as you can. Let your thoughts go where they go— follow your instincts. If you get stuck, keep repeating a word or idea until you get *un*stuck. For exam-

ple, write "I'm stuck, I'm stuck, I'm stuck" or "what next, what next, what next" a few times. Your brain will soon get bored with the repetition and come up with something more interesting to write about.

3. Don't edit. Forget about grammar, spelling, and other mechanical issues. The key to freewriting is to turn off your internal editor. This is easier said than done, of course. You may be so used to being evaluated on your writing that it may be hard to let go and allow yourself to write nonsense and make mistakes. But keep in mind that your freewriting is for your eyes only. That means you really *are* free to write just for yourself. You can abbreviate, use slang, use your own personal shorthand, write in your native language—whatever works for you. So jump in and let go. You'll have plenty of time to clean up your ideas later. For now, your goal is just to generate those ideas.

4. If you're more comfortable at the keyboard than with a pen and piece of paper, try freewriting on the computer. If you're a good typist, you can turn off or dim the monitor so that you're not tempted to edit as you write. The same guidelines apply: Reread the assignment and then write nonstop for five or ten minutes. Don't stop, and don't edit.

A Student's Freewriting

For example, one student received the following writing assignment:

Adrienne Rich wrote, "Lying is done with words and also with silence." Do you agree? Use your personal experience and/or your observations to support your answer.

Here's what the student wrote during a short freewriting session:

Do I agree? I think so. Is it a lie if you don't say something when you know something? Not technically but it has the same effect, doesn't it? I remember when I saw Jay with someone else but I didn't tell Karen. She never came out and asked me if Jay was cheating on her but I knew. But that's not really a lie is it so what do you call it? But there are more important cases where not telling the truth can be deadly. Like if you are HIV positive and don't tell someone before having sex. Or like if you know someone is going to commit a crime. Didn't someone just go to jail for not telling the cops she knew about the Oklahoma City bombing before they did it? But that's not a lie, that's just not telling, so not telling isn't the same as a lie. But it can have the same terrible consequences. I guess the point is that you know a truth but you don't reveal it. So they're not the same but they do the same thing. People can get hurt. Unless you believe what you don't know won't hurt you. But that probably falls into the same category as a "white lie." It's the other lies and other silences that are the problem.

Through her writing, this student came up with several examples and through them found a tentative thesis for her essay. She also has brought up some of the issues that will be central to her argument, including the definition of a lie and whether or not people have moral obligations to speak when they have certain kinds of knowledge. You can also see that the student has several run-on sentences, some repetition, and a very informal style. But that's absolutely fine. Remember, this is just her warm-up. Now that she has some ideas, she can get ready to work on her draft.

PRACTICE 1

Using a separate piece of paper or your computer, spend five minutes freewriting on the essay assignment below. Remember, there's no such thing as a wrong answer for this exercise. Keep your pen or pencil moving. Don't stop, and don't edit. Just write.

> *In his essay "Urban Strategy," William Rhoden describes a time that he put himself at risk to do what he thought was right. Describe a time when you, like Rhoden, put yourself at risk (physically, socially, emotionally, academically) to do what you thought was right. Was it worth the risk? Why or why not?*

LISTING

When you freewrite, you let your ideas come out as you move across the page in narrative form. With listing, your ideas come out as you move down the page. Instead of writing sentences, you write down words, phrases, or fragments that come to mind.

Listing is a terrific technique to use as a group if you have a collaborative writing project, but of course it also works wonderfully on your own. Like freewriting, listing is most effective if you turn off your internal editor. Don't stop, and don't edit. Set a specific time limit and try to write during that whole time. Like freewriting, you may be surprised at how many ideas you come up with. Here's an example of a student's listing brainstorm for his college application essay:

> *In your opinion, what is the greatest challenge your generation will face? What ideas do you have for dealing with this issue?*

The student's list went like this:
- Being overwhelmed by technology
- Staying in physical touch when everything becomes virtual
- How will we know what's real?
- If people live longer what about the generation gap?
- Taking care of parents—and grandparents
- Being overwhelmed by information
- What about people who don't have access to technology? Social inequality.
- The environment
- Are we using up our resources too fast?
- Are we running out of room?
- How can we recycle more?
- Alternate fuel, etc.
- World government?

- Diseases—new viruses, etc.—AIDS?
- What about our new power for destruction—biowarfare?

Notice how the student's list responded mostly to the first question in the assignment. Again that's perfectly okay. After all, he needs to know exactly what problem he's going to write about before he can propose a solution.

PRACTICE 2

Take three to five minutes to brainstorm a list of ideas for the following assignment:

There are many forces that contribute to our sense of self. What is a strong determining factor for your sense of identity?

_____

_____

_____

_____

_____

_____

_____

IN SHORT

Two effective ways to generate ideas are the *freewriting* and *listing* brainstorming techniques. Simply write non-stop about your assignment for a set period of time, either going across the page in sentences (freewriting) or down the page in a list (listing). Don't stop, and don't edit. The more freely you write, the easier it will be to tap into your creativity—and the more ideas you'll generate.

Skill Building Until Next Time

Use the freewriting and listing techniques for any kind of writing or thinking tasks this week. For example, if you have to buy a gift for a friend, brainstorm a list of ideas. Or, if you have to make an important decision, freewrite about that decision for five minutes.

L·E·S·S·O·N

MORE BRAINSTORMING TECHNIQUES: ASKING QUESTIONS & MAPPING

LESSON SUMMARY

This lesson describes two more techniques for generating ideas: asking questions and mapping.

Different people learn and process information in different ways. Some of us learn best by seeing; others by hearing; still others by doing. Some of us like a clear structure or framework; others think best when there are no constraints. For those who like structure, the asking-questions technique offers an easy, loose framework for generating ideas. For visual learners and thinkers, mapping may be the best brainstorming technique.

ASKING QUESTIONS

Like a reporter who asks questions to gather facts, you can use questions to generate ideas. The asking-questions technique uses six question words to help you formulate questions about the subject. The question words, known as the "five W's and an H," are:

who
what
when
where

why

how

Asking questions is really a modified form of listing, where every item in your list is a question. As with freewriting and listing, this brainstorming technique works best if you turn off your internal editor. Remember, you're still in the planning stage, so you're free to explore. There's no such thing as a dumb question, and there's no question you can't ask. Don't limit yourself to the five question words, just use them as a springboard to get you going. Here's how the asking questions technique might work for the following assignment:

Television is a very powerful medium. What do you think is the ideal place of television in our lives, and why? Explain. How close is the reality to that ideal?

- Who watches TV?
- How much TV do different types of people watch?
- What kind of shows are people watching?
- Does TV violence cause kids to be violent?
- What happens to kids who watch too much TV? How does it affect their schoolwork and relationships with others—parents, friends?
- Why do people watch TV?
- When was TV invented?
- Where do people have TVs in their houses?
- How many people have TVs in the kitchen? How does this affect family conversation during dinner?
- How many couples have TVs in their bedrooms? How does this affect their intimacy?
- How many kids have their own TVs in their own rooms? How does this affect their relationship with others in the family?
- How many families have more than one TV set?
- How many families sit down together to watch TV together?
- How many families talk about the shows they watch on TV?
- What do people expect from TV? Relaxation? Information? Entertainment?
- Can we trust information we get from TV?
- How much TV should a person watch? What kind?
- How can TV help us?
- How can TV hurt us?
- What about people who have no TVs? Are they less informed? More?
- What if we got rid of TVs?

Notice the number of questions this student was able to generate. If you look at the questions carefully, you can see how one question led to another—and this is precisely how a good brainstorming session should work. Once he got started, the student kept coming up with more questions—many that he probably wouldn't have thought of if he'd just stared at a blank page for a half an hour waiting for a good idea to come to him. Most of the questions begin with *how,* but noticed that he used all six of the question words.

Some of the questions are more relevant to the assignment than others ("when was TV invented?" for example, probably has little place in this essay). But clearly this student has a lot of ideas to work with. In the next lesson, you'll see how to use a brainstorming list like this to develop a thesis and organize ideas for your essay.

PRACTICE 1

Use the asking questions technique to generate ideas for the following assignment:

School uniforms for public school students is among the most controversial proposals for educational reform in America. Where do you stand on this issue? Defend your position.

_____

_____

_____

_____

_____

_____

_____

MAPPING

When you freewrite or list to generate ideas, your ideas develop in one direction—across the page (freewriting) or down the page (listing or asking questions). With mapping, your ideas can go in all different directions so that you can see your ideas in relationship to each other. Your map will show how one idea stems from another and how your ideas are related. Thus, mapping helps you organize your ideas as you come up with them.

On the next page is an example of a student's mapping brainstorm (Figure 1). First, the student put the main topic or question in a circle in the middle of the page. Then she branched out into the main ideas that she came up with. From there, she generated more supporting ideas and examples.

"Write an essay which conveys to the reader a sense of who you are." (Columbia University application essay)

You can see that the student came up with three main branches of ideas—her role as sister and daughter, her role as pianist, and her role as a student. From her map, you can see how one idea led to another and how different ideas are related. That's one advantage that mapping has over the other brainstorming techniques. When you

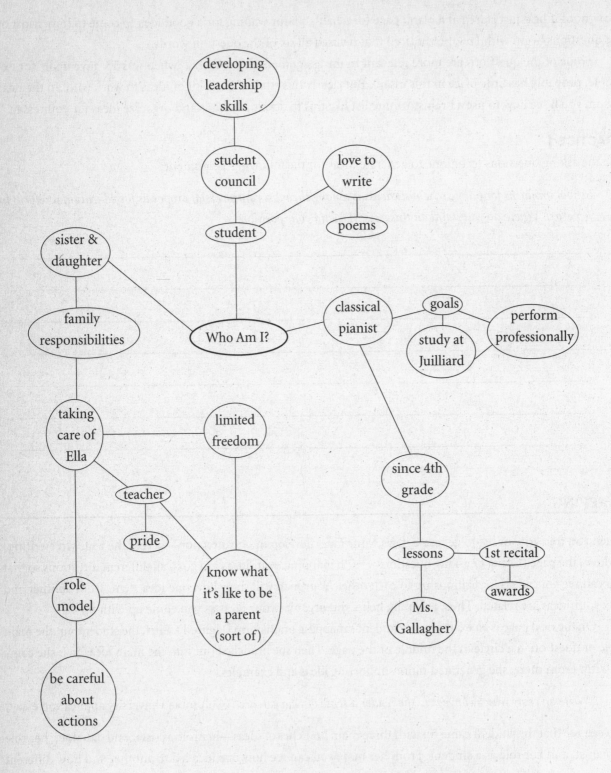

Figure 1.

brainstorm a map like this, you can see right away where your energy and ideas really lie. Clearly this student has much to say about being a big sister and classical pianist.

On the next page is an example of a student's map for a very different assignment (Figure 2):

Discuss how religion influences culture. Use specific examples from the religions we've studied so far.

PRACTICE 2

Use the mapping technique to brainstorm ideas for your own answer to the Columbia University application essay assignment:

"Write an essay which conveys to the reader a sense of who you are." (Columbia University application essay)

> **A Note about Outlining:** Outlining is another important essay planning tool, but it's generally most effective after you've already done some brainstorming and have developed a tentative thesis. The next lesson will explain what a thesis is and how to develop one. You'll learn about outlining in Lesson 6.

IN SHORT

To generate ideas for an essay, try asking questions using the five W's and an H: *who, what, when, where, why* and *how.* Or try a map: put your topic in the middle of a page and see your ideas develop in relationship to each other.

> ### Skill Building Until Next Time
>
> Use the asking questions and mapping techniques for any kind of writing or thinking task this week. For example, if you need to decide whether to join the drama club or get a part-time job, you can use the asking questions technique to help you come up with a list of pros and cons for each choice. Similarly, you could use the mapping technique to see how taking a part-time job would affect your life.

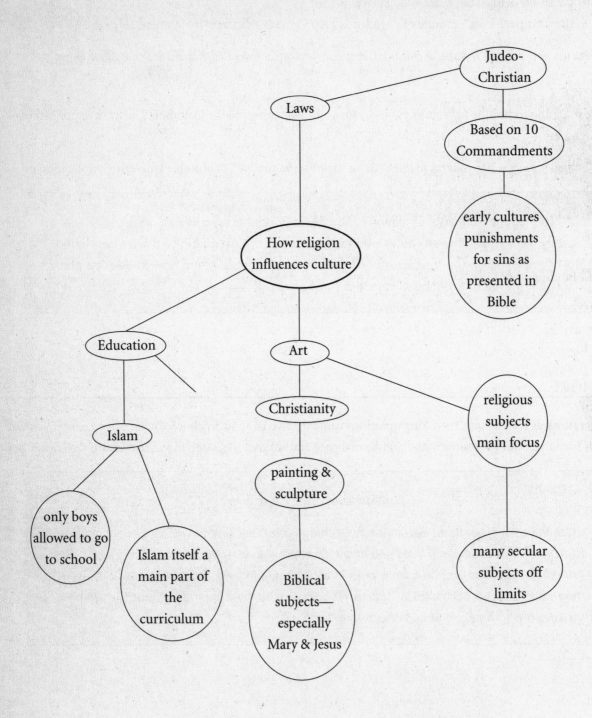

Figure 2.

L·E·S·S·O·N 5

CHOOSING A TOPIC AND DEVELOPING A THESIS

LESSON SUMMARY

This lesson explains how to narrow your topic so that it is sufficiently focused. You'll also learn how to develop a tentative thesis for your essay.

You've done some brainstorming and you've generated a lot of ideas. Now, how do you turn these ideas into an essay?

Perhaps the first thing to do is to accept that a lot of the ideas you've just generated will never go farther than your brainstorming sheet. In fact, it's a good idea to embrace this idea now: If you treat writing as a process—that is, if you plan, draft, and revise your essay—then much of what you write along the way will *not* be part of your final product. Writing is a way of thinking aloud and shaping your ideas into an effective piece of communication for your readers. You can think of the planning and drafting stages as rehearsals. Just as you want to rehearse your responses before you go for an interview, you need to rehearse your ideas before you give an essay to your readers. Even the best of writers don't get it right the first time. And once your essay is in the hands of your readers, there's nothing you can do if your readers don't understand what you're saying or aren't convinced by your argument. What you give to your readers needs to be clear and effective, and the fact is, it will take several attempts to get it that way.

So, the bad news is, a lot of your ideas are destined for the dustbin. But the good news is that somewhere on your brainstorming sheet is a great idea (or two, or three) that you can develop into an effective essay.

RULES OF THUMB FOR CHOOSING A TOPIC

Writing is really about making decisions, and here's the first major decision you have to make: what to write about. To help ensure that you make a good choice, follow the four rules of thumb listed below. The topic you choose:

- must be interesting to you
- must fulfill the assignment
- must be sufficiently focused
- must be able to be turned into a question

CAPTURING YOUR INTEREST

The first rule for choosing a topic is simple: *Make sure it's one that's interesting to you.* If it's not interesting to you, it's not going to be interesting to the reader. Your lack of enthusiasm will come across in your writing, and your essay is likely to be dull, dry, and uninspired. What you find a chore to write will also probably be a chore to read. But if your topic is interesting to you, then you can make almost anything interesting to the reader. The passion you feel for your topic will come through in your writing. Your readers will be drawn in by your lively prose and passionate assertions.

So as you brainstorm and consider your options, eliminate topics that don't interest you at all. You should also eliminate ideas that you would be uncomfortable writing about because they're too personal or because you don't have sufficient evidence to support them. Then, mark the ideas that excite you the most. Which topics do you find most interesting?

FULFILLING THE ASSIGNMENT

The second rule for choosing a topic is also basic: *Make sure your topic fulfills the assignment.* As you learned in Lesson 2, like it or not, you have to do what the assignment requires. That means you should eliminate ideas that don't fulfill the assignment, even if they're the ones that interest you most.

But what if you aren't really excited about *anything* you came up with in your brainstorm? What if the assignment is about a subject you just can't warm up to?

In that case, you have a challenge ahead of you. But it's not an insurmountable one. Your job is to find some angle, some approach to the subject that *does* interest you. For example, imagine your Contemporary American Politics professor has asked you to write an essay about a health care policy issue—something you've never really thought or cared much about. On your first brainstorm, you come up with a bunch of ideas, but nothing interesting enough to keep you writing for five pages. In that case, your best bet is probably to brainstorm again, using a different brainstorming technique. And this time, before you begin, make a short list of some of the things that *do* interest you. Even if they seem totally unrelated to the subject, you may be able to make a connection. For example, one student listed the following five areas of interest:

- music
- driving
- skiing
- Stephen King novels
- the Internet

Then she saw several possible connections. She could write about health care coverage for music therapy, health care policy resources on the Internet, or how accident statistics affect health care policies.

FINDING A FOCUS

Essay assignments will often ask you to write about a very broad subject area. For example, you may be asked to write an essay about the cold war or about heroes. These are very general subjects. Even if you're asked to write about a specific novel, that's still a pretty broad subject area—there are countless aspects of the novel you could address.

To write a successful essay, you need to *make sure your topic is sufficiently focused.* Take the subject of genetic engineering as an example. If you try to write an essay about such a broad topic, you'll end up frustrating yourself and your reader. You'll find that there's so much to say that you should really be writing a book instead of an essay. And since there is so much to say, you'll end up with an essay that barely scratches the surface of any single issue. A more effective essay would focus on a specific topic within that broad subject area, like one of the following:

Genetic engineering

↙ ↓ ↘

to find cures for diseases   to create "super" crops   for family planning (designing children)

It's far better to cover *one* aspect thoroughly than to attempt to cover everything topically. Think of it this way: What is more satisfying—having dozens of acquaintances or having a few very close friends?

Sometimes it will take several steps to get to a topic that is sufficiently focused. Here's an example of how one student narrowed her topic to find a clear focus:

Assignment:	Write a statement for your generation.
Broad topic:	My generation
Narrowed topic:	My generation's beliefs
Further narrowed topic:	My generation's beliefs about work
Sufficiently narrowed topic:	My generation's beliefs about the right balance between work and play

It took her three steps, but her third topic—"My generation's beliefs about the right balance between work and play" has just the right level of focus for an effective essay.

TURNING YOUR TOPIC INTO A QUESTION

The fourth rule of thumb for choosing a topic is that *it must be something you can turn into a question*. And not just any question, but one that will help you develop your thesis.

WHAT IS A THESIS, ANYWAY?

A thesis is the main idea or point of an essay. Generally, it is an answer to a question you have about your subject. It is also an opinion–the claim or assertion you are making about the subject which the rest of your essay develops and supports.

In the example above, the student narrowed her topic to "My generation's beliefs about the right balance between work and play." Well, what *are* her generations beliefs about the right balance between work and play? There are many ways she could answer this question. Her answer will state what *she* thinks her generation believes. And because it's her *opinion*, she will have to support it with evidence. Her answer to this question, in other words, will be her thesis. And her answer might be something like this:

"My generation believes that life should be equal parts of work and play."

The answer this student gives to the question now may not be the answer she puts forth in the final version of her essay. Because we discover what we think and how we feel through writing, writers often change their thesis as they draft and revise. After thinking on paper about an issue, you may realize that you feel differently than you originally thought. Or you may find that you don't have enough evidence to support your thesis. And that's okay. At this point, you just need a tentative answer to your question—something that can get you working on a draft. For now, a tentative thesis will do.

Here are two more examples of how students worked their way from an assignment to a focused topic, a question, and a tentative thesis:

Assignment:	Describe how you think the federal income tax system should be reformed and why.
Broad topic:	Reforming the federal income tax system
Narrowed topic:	Problems with the federal income tax system
Further narrowed topic:	Inequalities in the federal tax system
Sufficiently narrowed topic:	How to eliminate inequalities in the federal tax system
Topic turned into a question:	How can we eliminate inequalities in the federal tax system?
Tentative thesis:	Instituting a flat tax will eliminate inequalities.